OUR DANCE HAS TURNED TO DEATH

D1617978

OUR DANCE HAS TURNED TO DEATH

But We Can Renew the Family and Nation!

By
Carl W. Wilson

RENEWAL PUBLISHING COMPANY
1001 Virginia Avenue
Atlanta, Georgia 30354

ACKNOWLEDGMENTS

It is not possible to give recognition to all who in some way helped make this book possible. However, I wish to thank my secretaries, Juanita Hawley and Tina Crutcher, for their much typing. I am also grateful to Judy Moerlein, Lynda Whitaker, and Ballard and Puckett for art work.

Senator Sam Nunn read and approved the portions of the book regarding national defense. Others read the manuscript and made helpful criticisms. My wife has devoted the most time to editing and criticizing my views to help bring them more in line with the truth. Without her this book would not exist in its present form.

I am grateful to the publishers and government offices that have permitted the many quotes and illustrations. We have given credit in the notes at the end of the book concerning quotations we have reprinted with permission from McGraw-Hill Book Company; Times Books, a division of Quadrangle/The New York Times Book Company, Inc.; The William Andrews Clark Memorial Library, University of California, Los Angeles; Time, the weekly newsmagazine, copyright Times, Inc., 1979; the U.S. News & World Report, copyright 1974, 1977, 1979; Reader's Digest Assn., Inc.; Family Life Magazine, and others.

CONTENTS

Man's Leadership in Mammon Worship and the National Effects

Mammon Worship Distorts Sexual Roles and Threatens the Economy • Mammon Worship and Racial and International Tensions • Disintegration of Male Creative Work and of Labor Relations • Selfish Individualism Affects the Political Process • Selfish Individualism and Civil Injustice

Individualism Destroys Meaningful Marriage Benefits

Public Acceptance of Sex for Selfish Individual Pleasure • Resultant Male Attitudes Toward the Family • Women's "Lib" or Vulnerability?

Loss of Protection • Loss of Marriage Love • Loss of Desire for Children • Becoming a Matriarch or Gods • Not Freedom, but Double Jobs Requiring Superwoman • Motherhood Without Women and Women Without the Feminine?

The Breakdown of the Family

The Tragic Effects on Children

Neglect and Avoidance • Step-parents or One Parent • Children Battered, Rejected, and Aborted • Freedom from Parents • Child Worship • Parent Rejection • Child Exclusion • Crisis in Child Education • Child Neglect and Crime • Escape and Search for Identity by Drugs

Normalization of Homosexuality—The End of the Sexes and of Society

Conflict of Parents, a Main Cause of Homosexuality • Normalization of Homosexuality? • Conclusion

PART TWO: THE BIBLICAL TEACHING CONCERNING GOD'S CALLING TO MEN AND WOMEN IN THE FAMILY

FOREWORD

During my deep-water phase of parenting I found myself perched on a splintery seat watching a junior high half-time show—a parable of contemporary life. The young band marched on the football field and then, like a clip from a crazy dream, they crossed signals. Tubas bumped into cornets and drums floundered over french horns. Whistles blew and the drum major gesticulated, but order would not come and the embarrassed kids withdrew to the sideline in the laughing uproar of an amused crowd.

With genuine terror I now find myself marching with myriads of well-meaning fathers, husbands—leaders of this generation—who cannot discern signals. Everyone seems to be disturbed—even panicked—at the disarray of family and social life in the western world. Still we follow the wrong cues and retreat to the sidelines in defeat.

Confusion and ineptitude always stumble hand-in-hand over the backwoods of ignorance. From ancient days men of success and accomplishment inevitably perceive the "big picture." Old Testament history records that the sons of Issachar were men "who understood the times, with knowledge of what Israel should do . . ." Our need today is critical for men of their ilk.

Carl Wilson is such a man. With painstaking patience he has dusted off a path through history to trace whence we have come. He has sketched a grid to classify the enigmas of modern life. He has erected a cornerstone from the earliest institution of human life—the family.

Here is a free man's almanac, a guide for this year's cultivation based on past years' lessons.

Words about "getting it all together" are wasted unless they ride on action. To wander aimlessly lost in the woods is to squander energy and eventually to die. Carl Wilson's "Dance" has methodically taken the readings of our misaligned times. A book of substance in an era of surplus superficiality, it places in perspective what has happened and—more importantly—plots an escape route. Everyone of us—by virtue of family relationships—holds in our power a piece of the puzzle. I recommend that you read—and act upon—Wilson's solution. It is more than man's conclusion; it is God's answer and it makes sense.

HOWARD G. HENDRICKS
Dallas, Texas
November 1979

INTRODUCTION

I believe this is a very urgent message for America—perhaps the most urgent. This book has covered many subjects in a great many fields. No one can be an expert in so much, and I make no pretense at being an authority in all these areas. However, I have referred to and quoted studies relevant to most topics. Many views expressed are admittedly controversial. The value of my argument is in showing that all of the various areas of life are related and when properly interpreted support the main thesis.

That thesis is that the family, with traditional religious roles for men and women in a life-long monogamous marriage relationship, is the abiding natural foundation for social order, happiness and stability. When that view is abandoned for selfish individualism the society will collapse and die. I see the initiating cause as being man's distorting his role, which then initiates family decline. I hold that renewal of society must therefore begin with men.

I am researching for a much longer, more technical, and better documented work on the Christian view of history, which I hope to publish in a few years. This present book is a quick popular presentation of one of the main themes of that work. I have taken some liberties here that I would not use if my intentions were more academic.

The very important subject of how the intellectual and educational movements in the West have affected the spiritual failure of the man and of all society has deliberately been avoided here except for a few brief insights. In the larger work I will deal more completely with the way the philosophical and scientific movements may have influenced decline. To try to include that here, as strategic as it is, would obscure the urgent argument concerning the crisis of the family and the nation.

This presentation on the crisis in the family is divided into three parts. The first part, which looks at the growth and course of the crisis, is the most interesting and easiest to read. Chapter Five presents the core of the thesis of this first part. The prior chapters lead up to and support this, and those following examine the resultant consequences. The second part sets forth the Hebrew-Christian norm which is the ideal from which we have turned and which we need to renew. That is in less contemporary language, but important. I have tried to show that there is a oneness of the biblical data in the second part with the facts of research and history which are presented in the first. The last part is a plan for renewal which can, with God's help, change America.

Unless you are willing to become involved, don't read this book. It lays before you a course of action and responsibility. To read it and do nothing may leave you feeling guilty of failing to do what *you* can. The action of many individuals is what will change the trends.

This book is not written in a spirit of judgment, but of empathy. I too have been wounded by the times in which we live. I share with many of you the tragedy of a broken home in childhood, and saw the tornado of evil described here destroy and harm those I loved.

I have also experienced the redemptive power of God's goodness. While this book is not a religious testimony, I have much for which I am thankful. God has given me a lovely wife and He has given us five wonderful children and two grandchildren. But I have learned much through my own failures and through the failures of others who have trusted me to counsel with them about their wounds experienced by the course of this age. May God use this to heal our hurts, our failures, and our nation. I have tried to speak a word in season to those who are weary.

CARL W. WILSON

Part One:

THE CRISIS WE FACE

Chapter 1

AMERICA THE BEAUTIFUL

Evidence of Providence

No nation has ever been more clearly born in the womb of providence and grown to such great beauty, strength and prosperity as the United States of America. Thomas Jefferson, though a deist, was not amiss when he suggested that the seal of the new nation should be that of the children of Israel being led by God's pillar of cloud by day and pillar of fire by night.

From a few struggling colonies comprised principally of stalwart men and women who came to these shores with deep faith in their hearts and hope that their free worship might be accompanied by prosperity from hard work, the United States arose to be the most powerful and influential nation of all time.

This is not meant to imply that the United States has stood in a relationship to God that is unique from other nations in the way that the Bible claims for Israel. The thesis of this book is that every nation is answerable to God and can receive His help if the people seek it. I believe the leadership of the United States did seek the Lord in the first two centuries and that they received His help as few other people in history have.

God's goodness has many times been manifest. The birth of the nation was a near miracle to one with the eye of faith. Christopher Columbus pursued his journey westward against great opposition and discouragement because he felt called by the Holy Spirit of God to do so, and he named his first island in the new world San Salvador after the Savior to whom he attributed his success. It was hardly an accident that this event occurred at the very time that a young lad named Martin Luther was beginning to reach the age of consciousness of the moral conflict within man. Such timing made it possible that when religious persecution because of biblical faith reached a climax, the way to the new world had been widely known, offering a door of hope to those oppressed.

Was it by chance that world affairs were so ordered that a few struggling, poor, ill-equipped colonies could battle the mighty nation of Britain and gain their freedom? George Washington did not speak words of rhetoric when upon his resignation from the post of commanding general of the army he referred to the obvious working of providence in his significant victories. When confusion reigned at the Continental Congress, Benjamin Franklin called the gathering to prayer, and one of the noblest documents for mankind, the Constitution of the United States, emerged from those deliberations.[1]

The blessings of youth for the nation are also manifest. Just at the time when the muscles of business, industry, agriculture and commerce were growing strong, the opportunity to develop into a mighty nation extending from shore to shore emerged. At just the time when the nation was able and desiring to expand, conditions were ripe so that we could buy half a nation, the Louisiana Purchase, from a desperate Napoleon for only fifteen million dollars. If this nation had been confined to only the territory and resources of the eastern seaboard, would it have become so mighty? Was this an accident or the hand of a good God?

Did we not remember our Creator in the days of our youth so that we were led by righteousness and truth?

The foundations of our education were laid on the truths of God. The Puritan founders gave one of our foremost institutions, Harvard University, the seal of an open Bible with the word "veritus" ("truth") inscribed across it. Seventeen of the first eighteen universities and colleges were founded by the church or the church and state together, and eighty-five percent of our higher educational institutions were still guided by the light of Christian philsophy until after the Civil War. While it is true that the onslaughts of unbelief were felt even before the Declaration of Independence, our forefathers for the most part led the schools back to their religious origins time and again.[2] Thus our teacher has been the Lord God as our country has matured. From the halls of learning came an ethical people who could trust each other, who were not afraid of work, and for whom therefore free enterprise was a workable road to prosperity.

And in our prime of life we have found ourselves equipped and guarded for victory over our enemies. Isolated by two great oceans, we have had sanctuary that gave us time to build our strength and form alliances that helped us to be victorious in two great world wars. We had the time, technology and raw materials to build ships, tanks, planes and explosives superior to others. The United States was the first to build the atomic bomb only because of the aid of Einstein, Edward Teller, and others of scientific genius who sought sanctuary in our shores.

Riches of God's Goodness

What greater blessings have been bestowed upon a people? Today the riches of the average American are awesome. Solomon's wealth was not equal to most of ours. He never rode in a chariot pulled by as much horsepower as a Cadillac, Lincoln Continental, or Chrysler Royal—or a mere Pinto or Chevette, for that matter. No servant could light the lamps in his rooms as quickly as we can by the snap of a finger against a switch. What panoply of entertainment could he have assembled with such variety as performs before us on our numerous television channels? Foods requiring only minutes of preparation may be pulled from boxes, cans, and freezers and placed on our tables, that Solomon's feasts would hardly equal. Solomon's baths and toiletries served by hundreds of servants could not supply the convenience, cleansing and aromatic fragrance of the modern bathrooms. His speediest courier for communication would hardly be upon his horse in the time we can talk by telephone to the other side of the world. The wealth of America transcends that of any place any time in history.

What other nation has at times so graciously shared its wealth with others? The Marshall Plan helped Europe to rebuild by hard work to prosperity equal to our own. Our benevolence to our enemy Japan under General MacArthur's administration has led to great wealth for her. Our gifts and loans to many of the poorer nations of the world have been more than generous. Christian missionaries have taken Christian truth and education, helping people all over the world.

Americans have been known the world over for their prosperity and wealth. Many have come to our country for education and opportunity. The American people generally have experienced very little suffering and depravity; the nation has enjoyed great joy and dancing under the blessings of God.

Most important of all, our nation has enjoyed more freedom than any other on earth. U. S. citizens still enjoy the right to elect their leaders, to choose their own work, to have freedom of expression, and to worship the god of their choice in the way they please. Most of the nations of the world are under some form of controlled society.

Many nations formerly democratic have become dictatorial or socialistic within the last twenty-five years.

Civil Religion Recognized
by Our Early Forefathers

The founders of the American republic were aware their good fortunes were not wrought by human hands alone and that the people were answerable to God. Early the coins began to bear the official motto, "In God We Trust." Thanksgiving to Him was frequently expressed by our forefathers. Edward Winslow, writing to George Morton to invite him to the first thanksgiving feast called by Governor Bradford at Plymouth, said the purpose was to remember that "by the goodness of God, we are far from want." For many years the autumn feast of ingathering served as a time of thanksgiving.

In 1784 President George Washington proclaimed the first national thanksgiving feast. He called it "a day of public thanksgiving and prayer . . . to the great Ruler of nations for the manifold and signal mercies which distinguish our lot as a nation." Among the mercies, he referred to "the constitutions of government which unite . . . and establish liberty with order. . . . The preservation of our peace," and "The prosperous condition of our affairs, public and private." President Washington expressed concern that God "imprint on our hearts a deep and solemn sense of our obligations to Him for them; to teach us rightly to estimate their immense value; to preserve us from *the arrogance of prosperity* and from hazarding the advantages we enjoy by delusive pursuits, to dispose us to merit the continuance of His favors by not abusing them. . . ." (italics mine). This observance of thanksgiving has been made an annual affair by our presidents since 1863.[3]

That there was a national civil religion based on a common theism was evident in that successive leaders on numerous occasions called the people of the nation to repentance, prayer, and fasting. Like Washington, they recognized that disobedience to the Almighty was our greatest enemy. On July 12, 1775, the Continental Congress had said, "Taking congnizance of the present critical, alarming, and calamitous state of these colonies", it resolved that a day of "public humiliation, fasting, and prayer" be observed by "the inhabitants of all the English colonies on this continent" to the end that "we may, with united hearts and voice, unfeignedly confess and deplore our many sins and offer up our joint supplications to the all-wise, omnipotent, and merciful Disposer of all events, humbly beseeching Him to forgive our iniquities, to remove our present calamities, and to avert those desolating judgments with which we are threatened."

Winthrop S. Hudson, commenting on this resolution, said, "Confession of sin rather than a claim to righteousness, a pointing to one's own iniquity rather than to the iniquity of the enemy, seems a curious way to solicit divine aid and nerve men for battle. But strange as it may seem to us, the ritual of humiliation and fasting did not seem strange to members of the Continental Congress."[4]

Such fast days were observed with periodic regularity in the colonies throughout the American Revolution. These calls to self-abnegation and humbling continued frequently thereafter through the time of the leadership of James Buchanan, Abraham Lincoln, and Andrew Johnson. When Lincoln proclaimed a day of fasting he said, "Sometimes it seems necessary that we should be confronted with perils which threaten us with disaster in order that we may not get puffed up and forget Him who has much work for us yet to do."

The profound sense of God's sovereignty in national

affairs pervaded the thinking of the people and was expressed in great revivalistic movements. During the great financial panic of 1857–58 there were spontaneous gatherings of thousands of business men across the nation for noonday prayer and confession.

The Decline of the National Civil Religion

Washington's fear of "the arrogance of prosperity" that would cause the people to become "puffed up and forget Him," as Lincoln put it, began to be America's experience in the nineteenth century. It developed over many years and finally has obscured the vision of moral obligation, like a slowly growing cloud that ultimately shuts out the sun's rays.

From the very beginning the blind destructive aspect of human nature was evident. Even Christopher Columbus, whose explorations planted the seed to germinate the nation, allowed perversion of his divine leading to aspirations of pride and greed, and his glorious fame crumbled to shame and poverty. The noble aspirations of helping the Indians, often expressed in the early colonies, at times were overcome by abuse.[5] At no time has human nature been without its dark side.

But the historical record indicates that the mist for the cloud to cover our vision of obligation to God began to form in the 1800's, and by the end of the nineteenth century it began to obscure the light of divine will. By the second quarter of that century various theological perversions from the Hebrew-Christian traditions, such as Universalism, Unitarianism, et al., began to be popular and spread, and social abuses in the North and South grew. Then the Civil War broke, and brothers shed each other's blood in torrents, tearing the national unity apart. In that time many leaders interpreted this as a divine warning. That widespread sense of our moral obligation to God has now in the last quarter of the twentieth century virtually disappeared. As Hudson and Trinterud have said, "Civil religion had as its focus the nation and the nation's relationship to God. This is a distinction twentieth-century Americans find difficult to grasp. While maintaining rituals of national piety, most Americans have been schooled to think of religion in either ecclesiastical or *individualistic terms. . . .*" (italics mine).[6]

To be sure, many politicians have referred to our noble traditions. John F. Kennedy in his inaugural address said, "In American political theory sovereignty rests, of course, with the people, but implicitly and often explicitly *the utlimate sovereignty has been attributed to God. . . .* The will of the people is not itself the criterion of right and wrong. There is a higher criterion in terms of which this will can be judged." In Lyndon B. Johnson's 1965 inaugural address he warned us that "the judgment of God is harshest on those who are most favored," and that the United States has no promise from God that its greatness will endure. Similar statements may be found in the addresses of Eisenhower, Nixon, Ford, and Carter. But who of these has dared to call the nation to fasting, confession, and prayerful repentance? It seems somehow incongruous with our age, even though more people profess to be Christians and believe in God than ever before.

The emphasis on the individual in contrast to social relationships has grown steadily. Also, belief in man's wisdom and ability has emerged, and confidence in biblical revelation, which furnished the basics for knowledge about God and eternal things, has diminished. Hence, secular humanism, or faith in this material world and man, has gained dominance over trust in God and the supernatural.

The benevolence of the American people and nation has been increasingly blighted by American businessmen who have exploited the natural resources of less developed nations, and our national diplomacy has increasingly been guided more by selfish advantage than moral right.

In 1941 the great historical sociologist Pitirim Sorokin warned us, "The tragic dualism of our culture is indisputable and is widening from day to day. Its soul is hopelessly split. It is a house divided against itself. The dark demon of destruction has been progressively rising over its creative angel. Hence the spread of the sinister blackout of our culture."[7] About 1958 Nathan Pusey, president of Harvard University, warned, "Secular humanism is marching across America virtually unopposed and threatens to destroy everything that we hold of value."

Thus the "arrogance of prosperity" seems to have destroyed our sense of obligation to "the Ruler of nations." National civil religion has been lost. Emergencies no longer cause us to seek God. The confusion of Vietnam, the energy crisis, and rising inflation do not turn us to repentance, confession, and desire for divine deliverance.

I am convinced that the crisis is far greater than most Americans realize. Our body is sick, and the vital organ which the cancer of sin is attacking is the *family*. The death of the nation will surely occur if therapy for healing of the family does not happen soon. This book seeks to analyze how our nation has moved so far into sin and away from God so quickly, and from that analysis to prescribe a way to renew the family and our sense of obligation before God as a nation.

Chapter 2

MAN'S PURSUIT OF WEALTH DESTROYS FAMILY AND SOCIETY

The Nature of the Coming Crisis

There is considerable evidence that the social fabric of the United States is unraveling and the nation itself is in danger. While superficially the family is considered important, the stable family is in jeopardy. As a consequence, American joy is turning to sadness and suffering. This book will help you examine the evidence for the social unraveling, see the cause of the tears of grief of multitudes of us ordinary people, and feel the growing hate. What can be the source of this spring that offers us such bitter water to drink?

I hope to show the main cause of the nation's troubles is that many men in America have turned from the worship of God and have selfishly distorted their role in pursuit of wealth and status, giving them an overexaggerated prominence compared to the role of women. In so doing, they have neglected their wives and children. Some women, following the values of materialism and status set by the men, have revolted against the role of wife and mother for their selfish individual rights, producing dislike, abuse, neglect and rejection of children, who become a hindering responsibility. This over-emphasis on the rights of the *individual* by men and women has spread the disintegration of *society* even further. Men have been the chief causal agents in role distortion, but some radical feminists, homosexuals and proponents of children's rights are now actually attempting to strike a fatal blow to the family by other selfish role distortions. The American family is becoming an endangered species, and this could lead to the decay and downfall of the nation.

In short, the men have turned to greed, which is idolatry, and this has led to role distortions that are causing the breakdown of the family, which in turn is causing the disintegration of all society. If present trends are allowed to go unchecked, American society is likely to give way to anarchy, bringing misery to all its citizens, and America could cease to be a world power even by the year 2000.

The great Harvard sociologist Pitirim Sorokin long ago pointed out that when a society gives way to a sensuous culture, when it distorts the male and female roles and indulges in sexual anarchy, it is nearing collapse.[1] When the family breaks down there is no school for learning law and order and no certain basis for loving and caring relationships. When individual rights take precedence, when the family and society give way, the nation will soon fall. Sorokin said, "This decisive educational role is well summed up in the dictum: 'What the family is, such will the society be'."[2]

The Spiritual Family is the Foundation for Society

Most of the great civilized nations have risen to greatness out of the patriarchal type family which provided leadership for their religious, civic and economic values and organizations. Certainly this is true of those nations of the Western culture.

Professor Michael Novak of Syracuse University, in

discussing the modern bias in America against the family, stated, "Yet clearly, the family is the critical center of social force. It is the seedbed of economic skills and attitudes toward work. It is a stronger agency of educational success than the school and a stronger teacher of the religious imagination than the church. Political and social planning in a wise social order begin with the axiom: *What strengthens the family strengthens society.*

"Even when poverty and disorientation strike, as over the generations they so often do, it is family strength that most defends individuals against alienation, lassitude, or despair. . . . One unforgettable law has been learned through all the disasters and injustices of the last thousand years: *If things go well with the family, life is worth living; when the family falters, life falls apart.*"[3]

It is generally accepted that our Western culture has its foundations in the philosophy and art of Greece, in the law and government of Rome, and in the Judeo-Christian religion. Yet we forget that those foundations were produced out of the patriarchal family structure of those people.

After several hundred years of darkness and sexual and materialistic decadence in the Mycenae culture the ancient Greek people emerged about the eighth century B.C. The earliest roots of the Greek people are not entirely clear, but it is evident that they had strong spiritual families with male leadership and an honored position for the wives. The family structure was the basis for their organization and education. The nature of the family was monogamous. Decisions were made on the basis of family beliefs in God and traditions. The people were divided into tribes—Ionians, Dorians, and Aeolians—according to family origins. Each tribe was ruled by a king, assisted by a council of chiefs who were select aristocratic family heads. Through a long process the representative democracy of the Greek assemblies arose from the aristocratic family structure.

W. G. Forrest has said, "The basic unit of the system was the family, in Greek an oikia—roughly a man, his children, and his grandchildren—this at all levels in society, except the slave. Above the oikia was a larger unit, the genos or clan, a number of oikiai whose members considered themselves the descendants of a common ancestor. A group of gene formed a tribe."[4]

The history of the Romans, their kinsmen, is much the same. In Italy, Etruria had left a political vacuum, this resulting from decay produced by sexual extremes characterized by its notorious phallic rites. The Roman republic grew out of deep loyalty to family structure and monogamous marriage. J. H. Vincent has said, "The internal history of the state through the first four centuries revolves about the resistance of a few patrician families to any encroachment upon their privileges and honors."[5] As with Greece, a king ruled, advised by a council or senate composed of 100 patricians chosen from three tribes—Ramnes, Tities, and Luceres—each being composed of ten wards or curiae. The wives of the leaders were very prominent in helping them.

In early Greece and Rome the religious leadership was closely tied to the family and civil leadership. The religious priesthood arose out of family leadership. The king was the chief religious leader. The family was also the source for economic training, both of men and women. The family was therefore clearly the basis of all social order.

All culture of Judeo-Christian origin is also rooted in the family. The individual was considered important because each man and woman was looked upon as created by God in His image. But the individual was shaped by and integrally tied to the family. This identity was so close that a great-grandson could be called a son. There are instances in which this is true down to the sixth generation.

The nation of Israel was born out of the family of Abraham. The early worship of Israel developed from the worship and understanding of God established by Abraham and passed on by his descendants. The nation's God was known as "the God of Abraham, Isaac, and Jacob." That worship was perpetuated after the Exodus by the priesthood of the family of Aaron. In essence, Abraham's family altar became the tabernacle and later the temple in Jerusalem.

The civil leadership was passed on from Abraham to his son Isaac. The subsequent leaders of the nation came from his son Jacob and the descendants of his twelve sons. It was usually from the oldest son that the title "elder" was derived. A number of elders then became the leaders of Israel in their local groups. Later one Israelite family, that of David, became the line of kings or civil heads of government.

The New Testament church saw itself as an expansion of the family of Abraham to all nations (Romans 4:11–13), and men who were good fathers in their homes were chosen to be the "elders" of the local congregations (I Timothy 3:4,5,12; Titus 1:6).

In Israel the economic trades of herding sheep or cattle, raising vineyards, and the like were continued through the family. The land was faithfully passed down from one family leader to the next. Every fifty years any purchased land was restored to the original family. The family was the center of Hebrew heritage. More will be considered about this later.

From this brief sketch it can be seen that the family was the basic school and source for the society, economics and religion of the Greeks, Romans, and Israelites. Those nations continued strong as long as the family structure was strong. As we shall see, that strength began to wane when skepticism and indifference toward the early dominant view of God came in and led to the pursuit of wealth.

All of the spiritual, civil, economic, political and social roots for the West have been in the family. This is certainly true of America. The earliest government and religious leadership was based on that of the fathers of the families. Monogamous marriage was the norm and the law. The earliest government of the Puritans centered in the powerful family leaders who formed the "Puritan oligarchy."[6] Arthur Calhoun has said, "The fathers adopted the maxim that 'families are the nurseries of the church and the commonwealth; ruin families and you ruin all.' The maintenance of family religion was universally recognized in early New England as a duty and was seriously attended to in most families. Daily the Scriptures were read and worship was offered to God. Fathers sought for their children, as for themselves, 'first the kingdom of God and His righteousness'."[7]

Every town had select men who by law were to enforce family morals and see that family government was upheld. They were also to see that parents educated their children and acquainted them with the civil laws.[8] The most prominent clergymen in the colonies often perpetuated this calling in the family, as with the Mathers of Massachusetts.[9]

The traditional family has continued to be the *main unit of society* until the twentieth century. Now many forces in the modern world are militating against it. The vital issue is: can Americans weaken and destroy the family and still continue the enjoyment of the liberties and values that have been based on it? Can our society continue without its *foundation?*

At the conclusion of the article by Michael Novak referred to earlier in this chapter, he says, "For apart from millions of decisions by couples to bring forth children they will nourish, teach and launch against the void, the human race *has no future*—no wisdom, no advance, no community, no grace—only the emptiness of solitary space, the dance of death. It is the destiny of flesh and blood to be familied."[10]

The Urgency of the Crisis

Conditions are becoming urgent. Radical feminists and their humanistic supporters are working to remove legally all male leadership and establish a matriarchy. Homosexuals are striving to present homosexuality as a "normal" way of life. Pro-children's groups used the International Children's Year in 1979 to promote the idea of freeing children from parental authority. As we will demonstrate, Communists know what the dissolution of the family means, and they and other subversive groups are also seeking to disrupt family life.

A White House conference on children was held in December, 1970. In the opening paragraph composed by the Forum on Parents and Children, a report to the President said, "America's families and their children are in trouble, trouble so deep and pervasive as to threaten the future of our nation." They also stated, ". . . Our national rhetoric notwithstanding, the actual pattern of life in America today is such that children and families come last."[11] If the problem was deep then, it has become exceedingly urgent now, a decade later. The 1980 White House Conference on Families authorized by President Carter can be strategic. At present the radicals are rushing to fill up the delegations at the state conferences, while the masses of moderate Americans are asleep. The radicals plan to use tax dollars of the government to their own ends.

Armand M. Nicholi II, on the faculty of Harvard Medical School and the staff of Massachusetts General Hospital, has recently said, "For several years now social scientists have warned us the family is disintegrating and will not survive this century." He pointed out that several writers and movements advocate destruction of the family. He asks the question, "Is there danger that the American family will cease to exist? I do not think so. . . . We do, however, have serious cause of concern—not that the family will disappear, but that certain trends prevalent today will incapacitate the family, destroy its integrity, and cause its members to suffer such crippling emotional conflicts that they will become an intolerable burden to society."[12]

The Solution to the Crisis

As has been mentioned, the main problem of the decline of the family in America lies in the fact that men have forsaken their responsibility for spiritual leadership and under self-deception have departed from practicing faith in God. The pivotal point in the man's failure is evidenced by the change from the worship of God to the worship of mammon. Until men renew their commitment to God and put their wives and children first, there will be no slowing of the disintegration of society. Women will continue to follow the materialistic values of their husbands and continue to forsake their homes.

Also, basic to this is a recommitment of men to a single standard of sexual fidelity in a life-long monogamous relationship. If women are afraid their husbands may forsake them for other women, they will hesitate to assume the responsibility of bearing their children. Children, who are a financial responsibility and a limit to selfish desire for freedom, will be unwanted and will become the object of abortion or abuse. A successful attack to reverse these trends must be focused primarily on the man's spiritual default and his consequent role distortion, and only secondarily on subversive groups. I believe a national movement to renew spiritually the traditional family is the only thing that can save America. While Communist and other humanistic groups are openly advocating changes to destroy the family, their efforts are appealing only because of the man's failure to be the spiritual leader.

In a very real sense the forces for righteousness are now in a goal-line stand against the forces of evil. It is time to wrest the ball out of the hands of the opponent and begin a drive in the other direction. Groups of Americans are fighting to prevent the passage of laws which would weaken the family, but much less is being done to change the trends. The team that is always on the defensive and never on the offensive seldom wins. An effort must be launched to change the trends in the family. Of course, we still need to defeat the attempts to change laws if the results will weaken the family. If legal victories are scored on proposals now pending that would weaken the family, it will be very difficult indeed to turn the game around so that the righteous will win. We need to review some of the advances antisocial forces have been making and offer a positive strategy for victory over them.

Chapter 3

EQUALITY, DIFFERENCES, AND FREEDOM IN SEXUAL ROLES

The Sensitive Problem of Sexual Roles

The relationship of men and women in sexual roles operates in a very delicate balance. In a society where people have a strong faith in God, men and women gain their sense of worth and security by the belief that God made them and is concerned about them. That sense of self-worth and security gives stability to the sexual relationships. Moreover, it motivates husbands and wives to have responsible attitudes and actions toward each other and their children. The second part of this book will look more closely at that (cf. Chapter Seven ff.).

There are ways in which men and women are equal. There are also important differences. Both of these factors affect the feeling of self-worth and identity that a husband and wife give to each other. Selfish infringement of either the man or the woman on the nature of the other can disrupt the sensitive balance of their relationship, seriously affect their happiness and the happiness of their children, and destroy society. When there is a loss of faith in God, a disruption often occurs. America is going through a serious sexual crisis because faith in God has diminished and the ways men and women are equal and different are not understood and respected.

The intent of this chapter is to try to look at the ways men and women are different, the ways they have equality, the meaning of freedom and how differences affect it, and the ways men and women distort natural differences and harm each other and their children. The documentation for those differences will continue in the subsequent chapters.

Equality and Differences

Similarities that Give Equality

Today the general equality of men and women is accepted and there is little need to argue about the ways they are equal and similar. They generally have the same capacity to reason, understand and communicate. Physiologically they are similar. They walk erect and have thumbs that appose the fingers, have the same number of chromosomes (46), have the same kinds of blood. These and others set men and women apart from animals. (cf. also pp. 142, 143.)

Many women today are fighting for something that is rightfully theirs—equality with men. At the center of their struggle has been the Equal Rights Amendment (ERA), seen by many as the key to their victory. But is the ERA really the final solution? I am convinced we need to go beyond it to make sure that not only women, but men and children also, are assured the roles that would best meet the needs of all.

The ERA itself may be part of the problem since it deals with some areas while ignoring others. It distorts the differences between men and women, implying they should be the same in every way. If this distortion becomes a part of the U. S. Constitution, it will be difficult to correct. I will be referring in the succeeding chapters to evidences from history, anthropology, sociology and psychology which support the differences and show that such distortion of them can hurt all in society, including women.

Women today have difficulties to overcome, but there are ways to overcome these problems without overlooking those differences. Later in this book specific ways to do this will be suggested.

The fact that there are differences obvious to anyone was brought out by Hank Ketcham's Dennis the Menace, who once said to his pal Joey as they looked at a new baby, "You could pass her off as a brother for quite a while yet, but when she starts to grow up, everyone will know ya lied."

As with Joey, our bias for personal reasons can lead us to lie about the sexual differences. But the consequences are far greater than just exposure and embarrassment— it may mean survival of freedom, society, and culture.

Obvious Differences

The modern feminist movement has rightly emphasized the equality of women with men. But they have minimized and distorted the very significant ways they are different and have made equality to mean "the same." This is usually done by finding conditioned exceptions of behavior rather than recognizing the general characteristics of most men and women under most circumstances. Some differences are obvious and undeniable while others, often implications of the obvious, can be clearly discerned by observation and analysis.

There are some obvious differences. The man has one external sexual organ with the generative testes, also external. The woman has larger breasts, more hidden genital organs, internal ovaries for producing eggs, and an internal womb for carrying and then bearing the child. The

woman's sexual design is more mystical and secretive.
The male is constantly able to produce many sperm and
build up a reserve that must find release. The female
goes through a month-long cycle to produce usually one
egg. The male has greater strength in his arms and legs
for the work of protecting, providing and controlling.
The female has wider hips and large breasts for carrying,
bearing and nursing children. The male has a stronger,
deeper, and more authoritative voice; the female has a
quieter, softer, more soothing voice. Dr. Paul Popenoe
lists the following differences:

"1. Men and women differ in every cell of their bodies.
   This difference in the chromosome combination is
   the basic cause of development into maleness or femaleness as the case may be.

2. Woman has greater constitutional vitality, perhaps
   because of this chromosome difference. Normally, she
   outlives man by three or four years, in the U. S.

3. The sexes differ in their basal metabolism—that of
   woman being normally lower than that of man.

4. They differ in skeletal structure, woman having a
   shorter head, broader face, chin less protruding,
   shorter legs, and longer trunk. The first finger of a
   woman's hand is usually longer than the third; with
   men the reverse is true. Boys' teeth last longer than
   do those of girls.

5. Woman has a larger stomach, kidneys, liver, and ap-
   pendix, smaller lungs.

6. In functions, woman has several very important ones
   totally lacking in man—menstruation, pregnancy,
   lactation. All of these influence behavior and feelings.
   She has more different hormones than does man. The
   same gland behaves differently in the two sexes—
   thus woman's thyroid is larger and more active; it
   enlarges during pregnancy but also during menstruation; it makes her more prone to goiter, provides

resistance to cold, is associated with the smooth skin, relatively hairless body, and thin layer of subcutaneous fat which are important elements in the concept of personal beauty. It also contributes to emotional instability—she laughs and cries more easily.

7. Woman's blood contains more water (20% fewer red cells). Since these supply oxygen to the body cells, she tires more easily, is more prone to faint. Her constitutional viability is therefore strictly a long-range matter. When the working day in British factories, under wartime conditions, was increased from 10 to 12 hours, accidents of women increased 150%, of men not at all.

8. In brute strength, men are 50% above women.

9. Woman's heart beats more rapidly (80, vs. 72 for men); blood pressure (10 points lower than man) varies from minute to minute; but she has much less tendency to high blood pressure—at least until after the menopause.

10. Her vital capacity or breathing power is lower in the 7:10 ratio.

11. She stands high temperature better than does man; metabolism slows down less."[1a]

The man is physically designed to be the aggressor and penetrate, while the woman is to receive and respond (women can't actually rape). After much activity the man deposits at one instant release 300 million microscopic sperm that all vigorously fight their way to try to unite with one egg waiting in a tube.

Differences in Sexual Response

According to studies by Dr. Herbert J. Miles, the man's sexual arousal may be by visible distant stimulus or intimate touch and is quick (one to three minutes). The woman's arousal is less stimulated by the visible but more by touch and often requires much longer (ten to fifteen or more minutes). Her arousal is more closely tied to a good personal relationship and a positive psychological feeling than is the man's. The man prefers to lead and to stimulate the woman, while it takes 82 percent of the women usually from six months to two years to learn to give part of their attention to their husbands by actions of participation. Eighteen percent continue to find it is necessary to concentrate on themselves alone and be passive.[1b] Generally the woman must focus on *releasing* herself, while the man must focus on *controlling* himself. The natural biology of the man demands activity, while that of the woman is more passive. The man has one main area for erotic stimulation while the woman has many. The male orgasm is localized while the woman's may have an effect in more than one area and even pervade her whole body.[2]

Woman's Sexuality is More Long-Term and Secure than Man's

The man's one sexual organ with one main area for stimulation involves his sexuality being expressed in the brief time involved in arousal and intercourse. George Gilder says, "A woman is not so exclusively dependent on copulation for sexual identity. For her, intercourse is only one of many sex acts or experiences. Her sexual nature is reaffirmed monthly in menstruation; her breasts and her womb further symbolize a sex role that extends, at least as a potentiality, through nine months' pregnancy, childbirth, lactation, suckling and long-term nurture. Rather than a brief performance, female sexuality is a long unfolding process. Even if a woman does not in fact bear a child, she is continually reminded that she can, that she is capable of performing the crucial act in the perpetuation of the species. She can perform the only act that gives sex an unquestionable meaning, an incarnate result. Thus, regardless of any anxieties she may have in relation to her sexual role and how to perform it, she at least knows that she has a role of unquestionable importance to herself and to the community."[3]

Seymour Fisher agrees, "It was my conclusion, after reviewing all available studies, that the average woman is more 'at ease' with her own body than is the average man. . . . Her body makes sense to her as one of the prime means to become what she wants to become."[4]

The Sex Act Has Greater Importance and Risk for Men

Moreover, the man can fail easily in the sex act because he is the one who must perform, but that is not true with the woman. The man may fail at many points: he may fail to have an erection, he may finish too soon, he may fail to reach orgasm at all, he may fail to bring his wife to orgasm, or he may lose her to another man. "The essential need to perform is alternable only in sexual suicide. There is no shortcut in human fulfillment for men—just the short circuit of impotence. Men can be creatively human only when they are confidently male and overcome their sexual insecurity by action. Nothing comes to them by waiting or 'being'. . . . In general, therefore, the man is less secure than the woman because his sexuality is dependent on action, and he can act sexually only through a process difficult to control. Fear of impotence is a paramount fact of male sexuality." The feminist "fails to understand that for men the desire for sex is not simply a quest for pleasure. *It is an indispensable test of identity,* and in itself it is always ultimately temporary and inadequate. Unless his maleness is confirmed by his culture, he must enact it repeatedly."[5]

Bachelors may be well-adjusted if they gain a sense of worth from meaningful employment in society. But often such a man finds his mind continually searching for a woman with whom he hopes to enact his manhood repeatedly.

According to Mary Jane Sherfey, Kinsey's colleague, and Masters and Johnson, "Women can both enjoy sexual relations more profoundly and durably and forego them more easily than can men. In those ways they are superior. Whatever other problem a woman may have, her identity *as a woman* is not so much at stake in intercourse. She has other specifically female experiences and does not have to perform intercourse in the same sense as her partner; she can relax and virtually always please him."[6]

The Man's More Insistent and Less Secure Sexual Nature

Because his identity must be repeatedly proven, the man is persistently a sexual creature. His mind is frequently turned in the direction of sex, and as we shall see, unless and to the degree he is involved in meaningful creative work, this becomes an insistent part of his psychology. Moreover, once he has begun pursuit and foreplay, he does not want to stop until he has reached a climax. As one of my friends used to say, "The man has a tiger in his tank." It is not just because he wants the pleasure, but because he must prove his manhood and affirm his identity.

This is not true of the woman. Her identity by sex being broader, more obvious, more long-range and more secure, she does not need sex as much and orgasm is not as important to her. Midge Dector has said, "Women lack the kind of importunate, undifferentiated lust that infects most all men."[7]

This is why many see some reason for the double standard. The famous woman psychiatrist of the New York State Institute and Hospital, Dr. Marynia Farnham, long ago argued the double standard for men was understandable.[8] Gilder takes this position,[9] as do others. Clellan S. Ford and Frank A. Beach, in a cross-culture study of 190 different societies, show facts that support the male's naturally more aggressive and insistent nature in sex in order to seek identity. In almost every society men are far more promiscuous, more inclined to masturbation, to homosexuality, and to immodesty.[10] This is also supported by the multimillion-dollar pornographic market and the many topless and nude bars that cater almost exclusively to men. Only in rare cases do you find these female oriented, and these involve only a small number of women. The sexual rituals among primitive tribes are almost exclusively conducted by men and are another evidence. Pornography, and sometimes sexual ritual, are forms of sexual fantasy found most frequently among men who do not have access to abiding female relationships and because of inhibitions resulting from hostilities toward women.

Men Prefer a Continuous Relationship for Maximum Identity

Most men prefer a continuous relationship with a woman, even though they may settle for a short-term one to satisfy their persistent sexual drive. The majority of men want to marry a virgin, because a woman who has maintained her virginity is obviously not as likely to give herself to other men. Even in America's liberated age with available sex, most men prefer marriage. A woman's continual sexual relationship with him gives him the deepest sense of identity. Her continual submission to him sexually not only gives him immense pleasure but a sense of importance in that she repeatedly allows him this exclusive privilege. It is a form of respect. But a man wants more—he wants the satisfaction that he is able to bring his wife to enjoy full orgasm. In so doing she has fully humbled herself and given herself to let him give her this pleasure. Dr. Marie Robinson gives the testimony of some clients. One said, "I feel like a man again. No matter what anybody says, your wife's response is the most important thing, and it's got to be a response *in* intercourse. If she doesn't respond that way, you gradually lose faith in yourself and then you lose interest in making love."[11]

Men need this for their sense of self-worth. "Unless they (men) have an enduring relationship with a woman— a relationship that affords them sexual confidence—men will accept almost any convenient sexual offer."[12] The Playboy philosophy of preference to promiscuity is appealing to the male who has been denied a satisfying long-term relationship or who has a perverted image of women. A man usually prefers a continued exclusive relationship also because that is the only way he can be assured the woman will give him the recognition that a child she conceives is his. If he has had a continued exclusive relationship, he has a reasonable claim to paternity. If the woman has been with other men, he does not.

In conclusion, the woman's sexual power is greater than the man's. His is tenuous; hers is more assured. His sexual pattern and rhythm is short and concentrated; hers is long and pervading.

Brain and Psychological Differences Shown in Studies

Richard Restak, neurologist at Georgetown University School of Medicine, has gathered data from recent studies on men and women. He states, "Undoubtedly, many differences traditionally believed to exist between the sexes are based on stereotypes. But evidence from recent brain research indicates that some behavioral differences between men and women are based on differences in brain functioning that are biologically inherent and unlikely to be changed by cultural factors alone."[13] He refers to studies by Diane McGuinness, by Eleanor Maccoby, and Carol Nagy Jacklin at Stanford University and others.

Some of the differences generally found are as follows:

1. "Verbal and spatial abilities in boys tend to be 'packaged' into different hemispheres: the right hemisphere for non-verbal tasks, the left for verbal tasks. But in girls non-verbal and verbal skills are likely to be found on both sides of the brain." This affects their actions and reactions.

2. "From shortly after birth, females are more sensitive to certain types of sounds, particularly to a mother's voice," but also to loud noises.

3. Girls have "more skin sensitivity, particularly in the fingertips, and are more proficient at fine motor performance."

4. Girls are more attentive to social contexts—faces, speech patterns, subtle vocal cues.

5. Girls speak sooner, have larger vocabularies, rarely demonstrate speech defects, exceed boys in language abilities, learn foreign languages more easily.

6. Boys show early visual superiority.

7. Boys have better total body coordination but are poorer at detailed hand activity; e.g., stringing beads.

8. Boys have different "attentional mechanisms" and react as quickly to inanimate objects as to a person.

9. Boys are more curious about exploring their environment.

10. Boys are better at manipulating three-dimensional space. They can mentally rotate or fold an object better.

11. Of eleven subtests for psychological measurements in "the most widely used general intelligence test,

only two (digit span and picture arrangement) reveal similar mean scans for males and females. There are sex differences so consistent that the standard battery of this intelligence test now contains a masculinity-femininity index to offset sex-related proficiencies and deficiencies."

12. Girls who are "assertive and active" and can control events have greater intellectual development, while these factors are not as significant in male intellectual development.

13. More boys are hyperactive ("more than 90 percent of hyperactives are males.").

14. Because the male brain is "primarily visual" and learns by manipulating its environment, listening instruction for boys in early elementary grades is more stressful for them. Girls therefore tend to exceed them.

15. Girls do less well on scholarship tests that are more geared for male performance at higher grades.

It would seem that all of these findings tend to support the idea that men are generally more aggressive, more inclined toward planned organization and more likely to be interested in external environment while women are more people related and better at details in communication and at hand dexterity.

Social Implications of These Differences

The Woman's More Obvious Social Role of Childbearing

The differences between men and women are profound in their implications for building and maintaining community, society, and culture in the human race. The woman's social responsibility is obviously tied to her sexual physiology, namely, her ability to conceive, develop, bear, and nurse a baby. Her whole biology and psychology are involved in this. Her physical construction, her monthly menstrual cycle, her hormones, the fluids in her body, her body chemistry and the like are tied to it.

Moreover, having a baby is concealed and personal. Until recently, what went on within the woman was experienced mainly by her. The man is a bystander for nine months while she is the center of the creative drama. She experiences amazing biological changes to accommodate the growth and coming of the child. She experiences the movement and development of the baby while its father waits for her clues about developing events.

The social implications of women's role of bearing children are very great. The continuance of the human race is based on bearing children. The whole economy is based on the number of children born and their healthy growth. This determines how many houses and how much food and clothes will be needed, how many schools will be needed, how many workers will be employed, etc. The defense of the nation rests upon the number and quality of men for military service. The mother predominantly controls the psychological development of the child in its early years. We now know the influences of those years are important in determining the disposition, sense of security, etc., of the child, and this affects the kind of society formed.

The woman has an obvious claim to a parental relationship to the child. She carries, develops, then bears the child, and nurses it for several months. While the husband has an equal right to parenthood because his sperm initiates the baby's development and contributes half its genes, nevertheless his relationship is publicly unprovable. He is not involved with the child through the long process of its development, growth and nursing. He can claim to be the father only by the mother's designation. In a society of life-long monogamy this is done by the marriage commitment, and the father's claim is publicly accepted. Nevertheless, the mother's power to grant the right of paternity is supreme and exclusive. Also, the experience of being a mother and bearing a child is a tremendously significant act in which the man cannot participate. He is excluded from this awesome important and influential creative process that so profoundly affects society.

Dr. Margaret Mead has said, "Virtually nothing, though, in the whole set of male activities is equivalent to the finality of having a baby. . . ."[14] As Gilder puts it, "In childbearing every woman is capable of a feat of creativity and durable accomplishment—permanently and uniquely changing the face of the earth—that only the most extraordinary man can even pretend to duplicate in external activity."[15]

Man's Compensatory Creative Role as Defined by the Community

Because the woman has the overriding sexual identity, society has almost universally given the man the recognition of having the more important work to do outside the home. This seems to be given as a compensation for not being able to create children. Margaret Mead has said, "As far as I have been able to distinguish *in the whole of human history, the importance of male work is the most universal social difference between the sexes, aside from* the basic physical ones expressed in *reproductive activity*" (italics mine).[16] When work has been defined as men's work, it has been given increased importance. In one culture the women may do the same thing that men do in another (e.g., fish), but in the culture where it is man's work it is considered more important. Moreover, there is usually a certain mystery and secretiveness about men's work, comparable to the secrecy of childbirth.

Usually the man does the work in building the home and community. Most civilizations in their developing stage were led and constructed by men who had marriages that were monogamous with a high degree of fidelity.[17] This is usually done in seeking to provide for and protect the family.

The motivational factor in a man's work is love for his wife and family. Unlike animals, men and women have an abiding sexual attraction and a more continual power to reproduce (animals must come into heat). When a woman reciprocates love to a man who loves her, she concedes to him the continual privilege of sexual relations. When she conceives children in this love relationship she recognizes him as the father and expects him to provide for her and the children. For these privileges of identity the man submits to the long-term sexual patterns of the woman and devotes his creative work to her.

Woman's Desire for a Continuous Monogamous Male Relationship

The human offspring is much larger when it is born than offspring of the anthropoids but is much more dependent for a longer period of time. Its size is largely due to a larger brain. With a proportionately larger and more dependent offspring, the woman must lean heavily upon her husband in carrying, bearing and nurturing her child. The woman's desire for monogamy is heavily linked to her dependency in actually or potentially fulfilling her creative role as mother. Hence she normally subconsciously seeks to bring the short-term male sexual pattern in subjection to her long-term female sex pattern by offering or withholding her love. By her love she gains the benefit of his creative work to provide.

Two parents are required for properly raising the two children necessary just to reproduce the race. One parent may bear the responsibility, but he or she will have to hire a substitute parent to do part of their job. Both the man and woman may work outside the home, but again, the child will have to be turned over to a nurse, nursery or school where someone else serves as the parent while they are working. In a current national television interview with two lesbians living together, one with a child by artificial insemination was questioned about more children. She said she would like another child but she could not work and take care of two children. If government nurseries are established, unless enough productive labor is achieved by parents working to earn enough for the taxes to pay for them, the government will go increasingly into deficit to provide these substitute parents. In other words, the human economy seems to be gauged in such a way that two parents are unavoidably required to reproduce the race and continue civilization. A society may cheat on this only for a short while before it gets into trouble, because as we shall see, the motives for productivity decline.

Men Are More Equipped for Power to Lead and Provide

The man is more biologically and psychologically designed to do creative work outside the home, generally speaking. Women are weaker and more fragile than men. The running speed records in the women's olympics are comparable only to high school records for men. Women cannot compete in weight lifting or in the rougher contact sports such as pro football. Medical research shows that after having a baby, a woman athlete probably cannot do some things without causing hazards to her health. For example, Dr. Allen G. Charles at the Michael Reese Hospital and Medical Center in Chicago says many women runners cannot continue to jog without damage to the muscles that hold the uterus in position.

While a few exceptional women athletes may compete and win against less capable men in sports requiring skill and agility, they cannot generally do so against men in grueling, heavy, hard, and rough physical sports or work. They may play football in the midget league, but not in college or the pros. In the movies the women police do not corner the tough criminal and fight him in the alley. They usually use skillful karate or fight other women, which becomes more comical than heroic. In general, the evidence seems to be that men are more equipped to protect and to conquer nature and wrest from it provisions for living.

The man is more designed to be authoritative. His greater physical power and more authoritative voice equip him for this. A home cannot be run on a democratic basis effectively, especially if there are as many as two children. Even with only two people, one will become the leader. Dr. Marynia Farnham has said, "The more men and women are rivals, the less they are lovers. You cannot fuse these two pictures very easily. You cannot have in any animal society that we know of, a situation in which there is not a position of dominance and a position of non-dominance. You cannot have two absolute equals in one home. No matter what we like to think about ideally, this is not possible."[18] Traditionally in most societies throughout the world the men have been the leaders and organizers in creating culture.

As protectors, providers, and leaders in creating culture, men tend to organize. If it is to hunt animals for food, or fight a war, or build a building, or worship God, men find other men with complementary skills and get together to organize to do the job. In their consultations and planning they withdraw from women to do their work. Their hierarchies of leadership are therefore clothed with mystery and ritual that often are in private conference rooms and hidden from the public.

Male Recognition Required for Constructive
Social Motivation

Men in their aggressive leadership and organization
to create society and culture are equalizing their meaning
over against the social power women have in bearing
and raising children. If men are denied a distinctive and
socially creative role they will revert to the only ways
they can to gain identity—namely, by sexually conquering
as many women as possible and by using their superior
physical force in violence and organized military gang
aggression. Gilder says, "The role segregation (of men)
is not a function of economic utility; it is a reflection of
the sexual constitution of the community. Because of the
amorphous sexuality of males, they must be given specific
and exclusive tasks, not to accomplish the business of
the society but to accomplish and affirm their own identi-
ties as males. If such roles are not given them, they disrupt
the community or leave it, or else they subside into a
torpor, punctuated with rituals of sexual self-exal-
tation."[19]

The ego of the man *cannot happily* submit to the woman's sexual power and devote himself faithfully to his
wife and home unless she gives him a sense of worth
and identity. He needs an uncompetitive continuing faithful sexual submission and a meaningful distinctive role
in work that is socially constructive and is appreciated
by his wife and children. While he ought to be helpful
to his wife in her tasks and include her in his, giving
the baby a bottle, changing diapers, washing dishes, helping with housework and doing jobs that are more associated with the feminine role offer nothing distinctive for
the man. When women want to bring men into their
work or when women enter the work of men, they give
men nothing to compensate for their exclusive power to
bear children. Women may complain of the fragile ego

of men all they wish concerning this, but they are being dishonest in not facing the fact that they uniquely possess power that men have been denied. And this will produce maladjustment in men that will bring about undesirable social effects.

When the Russian Communists began to encourage women to become medical doctors, after a few years the medical profession was vacated by men and turned over to the women, except in specialized distinctive fields. It is not without significance that with the influx of many women in the American work force along with men in the same jobs, men have dropped out. "While female participation has risen to nearly 40 percent, the real male participation rate has sunk from almost 90 to just above 70 percent."[20] They have joined the criminals, drug addicts, alcoholics, and unemployment rolls.

When the woman recognizes and appreciates her husband's provision by creative work and when she offers him sexual love, he will be a hard worker with productive ingenuity. Her love shown through such respect will be a powerful motivator. Employers have long known that a good family man with a loving wife is the best type of person to hire. "If he finds work that affirms his manhood and a girl who demands that his sexuality be submitted to hers—submitted to love and family—he is likely to become a valuable and constructive citizen."[21]

Can Women Take The Male Aggressive Role and Society Continue?

It has been debated as to whether men are aggressive naturally or as a result of cultural conditioning. While Margaret Mead argued that aggressiveness was a socially conditioned characteristic for men and could also be learned by women (see her book *Sex and Temperament in Three Primitive Societies*), it is quite interesting that in her previous book, *Male and Female*[22], she admitted that the tribes were dying out in which she demonstrated that women could be aggressive. She also admitted that there was a loss of complementary character and social adhesiveness in those tribes. Ralph Linton, the great Yale sociologist, has also commented that the disappearance of dependent roles between the men and women in the West, especially the United States, may be the chief cause for divorce.[23]

Equality Shown the Wife by Communication and Her Assistance

Men and women are above animals in that they have the power of reason, can communicate logical ideas, can create culture and have a consciousness of right and wrong. There is no question that women are equally as intelligent as men and can learn almost any skill a man can and are better at some. Since women mature faster than men and their sexuality gives them a more long-range psychological outlook, girls are usually mentally ahead of boys in school and are more persistent and consistent in their studies. Because men are more doers it is harder for them to attend very long at tedious tasks. In coeducation classes the girls generally excel the boys, and for this reason coed classes can be demotivating for study for all but the brighter boys. Women can practice mechanical skills and do just about anything men can, provided it does not require great strength.

Therefore, women naturally want to be treated as equals in regard to their intellectual and other capabilities. A woman is generally happy and willing for her man to be the creative working provider and leader if he communicates about his work with her and if he involves her as a contributor to his work of providing. Judy Garland once put it this way in the article "How Not to

Love a Woman," "We want to argue with you, but we don't want to win."[24] In essence she was saying, we want to be recognized as your intellectual equal and to have our views considered but we are desirous of your leadership.

Women want to carry out their creative role of bearing and raising children, but they want this task to be appreciated for its great difficulty and significance both biologically and intellectually. The husband's communication with his wife about her problems in this area offers recognition of her equality. But she also wants to share insights about the world that can help him, and also about his work, especially as it relates to people and human relationships. In her intimacy with human development by rearing children she gains an understanding of human nature that men seldom achieve. Moreover, she wants to contribute as much as possible to the financial upbuilding of the family, and to helping him create culture.

The intolerable thing to a woman is to be neglected, shut out, not communicated with as a person of equal intelligence. She also must feel she can help as an equal partner and she must feel that her husband thinks that developing children in their character and in other ways is very important. If he does not communicate and treat her as a loving companion and give attention to the children, her role in sexual relations and having and raising children becomes intolerable. She will become constantly on the defensive and they will end up fighting. Her equality as an intelligent human being must be acknowledged by her husband or her sexual role becomes suicidal and she cannot bear it. With his communication her role becomes meaningful and motivating.

It is easy for a man to interpret the woman's role in the narrower meaning of her bearing and nursing children and homemaking. Her intellectual ability and skills need to be appreciated for what they can contribute both in and outside the home. Her husband is the chief person to motivate her and enable her to use these. His communication of encouragement and appreciation are exceedingly important to her for her identity and self-worth.

Conclusion

The common characteristics of men and women, such as their power of reason, the physical dexterity and skills that enable them to build culture, their ability to communicate ideas, their continuous sexual attraction, and a sense of right and wrong, all place them above animals. These similarities, as well as their differences, make men and women social creatures and distinguish them from all other living creatures.

The differences between men and women, with their implications for identity and self-worth, are complementary for living together and having and raising children. Dependence because of different roles is a social glue. Ignoring these different roles and seeking to make men and women the same is a perversion of nature and may destroy society, reducing men and women to the level of beasts.

The Created Limits of Real Freedom

People who are hurting and rebel to gain more freedom for themselves often have fuzzy thoughts about what real freedom is. There are boundaries to freedom resulting from our created natures. I would like to exercise the freedom to sing in public like my daughter who has a lovely voice, but my friends would prefer I didn't try. A dog may be free to be trained to walk on his hind legs alone, but if he does it constantly he will suffer. A man is not free to have babies and nurse them. A woman may act exactly like a man, but in time she will discover she has transgressed the normal bounds of her freedom and she will suffer undesirable consequences.[25] A child may want to be free from parental guidance, but unless he or she learns to submit selfish desire to concern for others, miserable maladjustment and psychological conflict can result for life.

The Commission on the Life and Work of Women in the Church of the World Council of Churches in 1952 published *A Study of Man-Woman Relationships,* which was written by Sarah Chakko and Kathleen Bliss. From this worldwide study they concluded, "There is a real danger for women in this equalizing process. Equal conditions of work and living do not guarantee woman's freedom, for *women need different conditions from men to give them equal freedom* with men. (This urgently needs elaboration in different national and cultural situations.)" (italics mine).[26]

The *New York Times* reported some statements by Carolyn Lewis, associate professor of journalism at Boston University, concerning a friend who had been criticized for resigning an exciting political post in Washington to take care of her new baby and to keep house for her husband. Mrs. Lewis shared her "growing uneasiness" about the women's movement. "In our eagerness to exact equal treatment, we women seem to be forgetting who we are. We are not men. Men cannot bear children. And for a woman, the birth of a child is a transforming experience.

"Of course it's great to write speeches for a senator, or design public policy for an education department, or work as an administrative assistant to a high-powered executive—but all of that can pale dramatically before the tender wonder of a newborn living creature.

"Here is a tiny talcumed ball of potential, the whole luminous future of the universe, waiting to be loved and shaped. There is nothing either inconsequential or demeaning about choosing to make this child one's life work.

"Nor is there anything shameful in wanting to make life comfortable and happy for another adult human, like a husband. There are good and useful and important things to do inside the home, and the women's movement makes light of the fact at its peril.

"I'm glad it is now socially acceptable to work outside the home. When I made that choice years ago, it was considered downright immoral. I'm glad today's woman can pursue a career free of stigma, if that's what she wants to do.

"But the world outside the home is not the only real world. The rewards worth having are not necessarily the rewards of salary and status. There are psychic returns in giving and receiving love, in molding a child's mind and spirit.

"It is true that we women have much to do to achieve equal treatment in the job market. That fight has to go on. But at the same time I sense a strident militancy that makes it harder for those women who prefer to stay at home. Parallel with the freedom to work outside the home must go the freedom to work inside it without being made to feel a pariah.

"It is good to see my friend choosing to stay at home, because that's where her heart leads her. But it is sad to see that making this choice, rather than another, is construed as turning her back on the women's movement.

"On the contrary, I believe my friend is quietly and courageously reminding us what being a woman can be all about."[27]

When a woman has a husband who lovingly provides and who maintains a kind but firm hand of discipline over the home, does it not really free her to be truly woman? She is released from fear of how her babies will be cared for so that she may joyously bear them. She can freely give her tenderness and nurturing care to the children without fear that they will make this softness a grounds for license to push her around because she knows the firm hand of her husband will see to their obedience to her will. She can help her husband with his work of providing, but be free to leave it to him at any time the children need care. Most women want that freedom to care deeply for their children. Many women who are seeking to raise children without a husband will testify to the difficulties they suffer without firm male discipline in the home.

Effects of Selfish Deviation from Sexual Roles

When selfish motives exalt the individual desires of the man or woman the delicate natural sexual balance is thrown off, with serious consequences to individual freedom and to society. Man's selfishness will lead him to distort his role, with adverse effects on his wife and children. Woman's selfishness will lead to her role distortion hurting her husband and children. In the end children hurt their parents and those who are later related to them. It is very easy for either party to be deceived into rationalizing that they are right in what they are doing.

The Man

It is very easy for the man to become selfish and distort his role. In his effort to earn money to provide for his family and to create a better world, he can separate his work and money-making from its objective of supplying for them. He forgets his great worth in the eyes of God, and in the battle of the marketplace and his effort to get ahead, he may seek to achieve the prominence of position and power by accumulating money for a sense of his own self-worth. He will then pursue money as an end in itself and, while he may supply more things for his family, he will neglect to spend time with his wife and children. Unknowingly he has separated his creative work from its family objective and ceased to lead the family as God created him to do. He has abandoned his creative work as a way of sexual identity that produces society.

He will then be afflicted with the "arrogance of prosperity." He will feel he is more important than his wife and children and overexaggerate the importance of his role and what he is doing. Wealth and power, like alcohol and drugs, produce a euphoria. He will deceptively think he doesn't need the identity from a long-range sexual commitment to his wife and from being a father. He will then not only fail to be interested in his family, but he will not communicate with them and begin to expect his wife and children to be subservient to *his* needs.

Being neglected, the wife and children will then react to his leadership. The wife will carry her hostilities over to their sexual relationship and fail to be responsive. Feeling unloved at home, the man will then spend more time in his work to seek to accumulate more wealth and more influence in the world so that he will have a greater sense of selfish worth. His time and communication with his wife and children diminish even more, and she will be more and more shut out from what he is doing.

Having turned away from God in the pursuit of wealth and material things, he then becomes more interested in the fleshly, the sensuous, and he becomes less concerned about what is right. He often gains a false sense of importance through accumulating wealth and may take his wife's love for granted and seek other women too. Or he may feel unloved by her and so look for another woman to conquer sexually. In his guilt he often turns to alcohol and drugs to help him relax. His physical health often is affected and eventually the rat race to gain more money loses all meaning. Moreover, his wife becomes bitter, loses respect, and is open to turn to other men. The children are raised in the midst of these hostilities; often their affection is competed for, and they are not disciplined, especially by their father. The father, having little relationship or respect, then may become dictatorial and use violent force to try to get obedience and respect. His motives for working (love for the family) are diminished and his productivity will begin to fall.[28]

This man may affect other men to pursue wealth with the same idolatrous greed. He infects others he contacts with his objectives and goals. Together they will affect others with whom they are involved. In turn, a whole economy may be affected and many families distorted.

A man may not be successful at gaining wealth and power, but if he gets caught up in letting *wealth* and success be *his goal,* he will still neglect his wife and children. In fact, his sense of failure where other men succeed may lead him to try to find identity through conquest of another woman. This often happens to men when they are in their forties and haven't achieved what they or their wives feel they should.

We have quoted extensively from George Gilder's book, in which he reviewed a number of anthropological and archeological studies about men and women and showed that when a man fails to find some identity in his work and in a leadership role he resorts to antisocial alternatives. He seeks to prove his male power by increased promiscuity, or he fantasizes or sublimates through sexual ritual (which in the United States would send him to male bars, nude joints, and pornography), or he turns to male group violence which allows him to demonstrate his superior physical power over that of women. By turning to war-like tactics, he seeks to find some meaningful role through his superior physical power. In many pagan societies this has come out in wife-beating as well.[29]

The selfishness of a man may be expressed in his physical sexual relationships with his wife in such a way as to cause hostilities. He may selfishly deny his wife the patient gentle preliminary love she needs. He may not seek to control himself but enjoy himself early and again leave his wife unfulfilled. He may consciously or unconsciously withhold his own fulfillment to make his wife feel inadequate. Worst of all, he may ignore her and not seek sex with her at all because of his bitterness or preoccupation with business. He may insist on birth control for economic or other reasons and refuse to let his wife fulfill her creative role in conceiving and becoming a mother. All or any of these selfish ways of acting can cause hostilities from his wife, or may be caused by them.

The Woman

The wife may deny her husband any sense of identity or importance. She may do this by earning more money than he or by competing to do so. She may criticize him and make him feel he is not keeping up with the Joneses and is not achieving as he should, thus exalting her role as adequate and his as inadequate. She may compare him to her father or other men in doing this. She may not allow him to be the leader in the home by refusing to submit to his decisions. She thus dominates the home, leading the children contrary to his wishes and even belittling him as a leader. She may do these things to compete with him because of her selfish insecurity.[30]

In sexual intercourse a woman may also offend her husband's manhood. If the woman is the aggressor and takes the initiative from the man, she may offend him, even to the extent of rendering him impotent. On the other hand, she may refuse to show any affection, but lie there indifferently rather than respond to his love by returning affection. She may even criticize him for his clumsiness rather than helping him and guiding him by touch or words. In these ways she shows her hostilities and makes him feel less than adequate as a lover. She may deny him sexual relations, thereby denying him not only pleasure but also a sense of importance by submitting to him. She may be unfaithful to him and seek sexual relations with other men.

As she sets the daily example of hostility and disobedience before the children, she teaches them rebellion. This rebellious attitude will be carried over to all other authority—rebellion against school authorities, against police and civil laws, and against God. Her failure to love and nurture them and to spend time with them will leave them insecure and seeking attention.

Role Changes and the General Effects on Children

As competition breeds conflict between men and women, this leads to selfish competition for the affection of children or to disliking or neglecting children. Hate breeds hate. Moreover, the attitude toward the opposite sex communicated by hostile parents conditions the child so that he or she carries preconceived prejudice against the spouse into his or her marriage, or gravitates to homosexuality.

When a mother's loving care and a father's loving discipline are lacking, the children are left insecure, unresponsive to authority, and undisciplined. Without controlling oversight and adult example, young people develop selfish individualistic, independent, antisocial attitudes and actions. These are reinforced by their peers. The result is increased criminal behavior.

As the crime rate in this country began to show a rapid rise, studies were done that indicated the distorted roles of men and women were related to it. Samuel S. Leibowitz, senior judge of Brooklyn's highest juvenile criminal court, concluded from his intensive search in various peoples of the world for the cause of juvenile delinquency, or lack of it, that there was one main solution. He said, "Put father back at the head of the family."[31]

Evidence from a number of physicians and clinical investigations clearly indicates that denial of maternal affection to children leads to retardation in physical development and even death, and to delinquent and criminal forms of behavior which carry over from childhood.[32]

These findings have been reinforced by Urie Bronfenbrenner and his associates in their studies in a number of nations. They found that the only country where children were more willing to engage in antisocial behavior than in the United States is the nation closest to us in the Anglo-Saxon tradition of individualism. Bronfenbrenner says, "England is also the only country in our sample which shows a level of parental involvement lower than our own, with both parents—and especially fathers—

showing less affection, offering less companionship, and intervening less frequently in the lives of their children."[33]

All the results of role distortion by men and women have profound social effects.

Chapter 4

HISTORY OF ROLE CHANGES AND THEIR EFFECTS IN THE U. S.

Introduction

In Chapter One it was asserted that the rise to power and prosperity in the United States was based on divine blessing as well as hard work. I presented evidence that the male leadership of our nation exhibited a real sense of dependence on God for those blessings.

In Chapter Two the thesis was proposed that the basic problem in the United States today lies in the family, which is the foundation of Western society. Moreover, I stated that the *key* to the problem is not rebellious women and the feminist movement, but first the failure of the American man. In Chapter Three I have tried to look at the ways in which men and women are the same and the ways they are different. Beginning with the obvious, we then sought to show the implications of these differences as reflected by studies and reasonable implications. It was found that the differences between men and women are important in finding a stable identity and in promoting society. It was concluded that selfish individualism by the man or woman can destroy that sense of identity and disrupt social adhesiveness. The assertion of *my* freedom, *my* rights, can destroy society and the freedom of everyone.

This chapter is a presentation of the history of the role changes of American men and women and their effects on relationships.

Role Changes by Men and the Effects

Men Forsook Spiritual Leadership

There is a paradox in American religion. The number of people in the United States *professing* to be Christians and belonging to the church has consistently *increased* since the nation's founding in 1776, while the man's *actual trust* in God and his spiritual leadership in the family has *diminished.* I hope to show there are indications that the male population has deceptively become hypocritical. Their personal trust in God in practical ways has declined. Hence, the national civil religion has declined and our nation has lost its moral direction and courage.

It is necessary to understand the events prior to the Declaration of Independence and the spiritual tensions at that time to understand this development. As was shown in Chapter Two, the early founding fathers of the American colonies had a strong commitment to God and worship was centered in the home. However, this soon changed.

After the victory of Protestantism in Europe in the middle of the seventeenth century the majority of the population in the United States became more and more unchurched. There were two main reasons for this. First, the nature of the migrating people changed. Some of the devout religious people returned to Europe. But more important, many non-religious people came from Europe to America to seek opportunity. For example, after Cromwell's victory in England, large numbers of the Cavalier class fled to America. So many godless people came into the colonies that some colonies passed laws to try to prohibit strangers from settling in them.[1] Moreover, even the most devout were tired of the religious conflict that had kept them trusting God. Thousands had died in Europe and all of life had been disrupted. Now that the right to worship God had been won—the Edict of Toleration had been passed in England and the Peace of Westphalia signed in Europe proper—people began to relax their commitment, their family worship waned, and they turned their attention toward improving their material conditions. Speaking of Massachusetts, for example, Wertenbaker said, "The religious zeal of the first settlers was less apparent in the second and third generation; the ministers commanded less respect and love; . . . the unity of church and state in the towns had been disrupted; despite all the efforts to exclude them, strangers had come in who were out of sympathy with the church and the government. . . ." However, "the ideals of the founders still exercised a powerful influence upon the minds and hearts of the people. . . ."[2]

All of the institutions had been founded on the Christian philosophy: the laws and courts were based on it, the educational institutions taught it, and most of the leadership in the main professions were Christians. But by the time of the Declaration of Independence only about 5 to 6% of the people were in the churches.

Hence, the church soon began the great revivalistic movement, commonly called the Great Awakening, to try to change this. The revival movement basically focused on calling the *individual* to repent and turn to God in Christ. The multitudes began to turn toward the church. The number of people in the church increased from 5% of the population until now about two-thirds of the people in the United States have some church affiliation.

While family worship continued to be important, it was affected by the revivalistic focus on the importance of the individual which was the outgrowth of the Protestant concept of the salvation of the individual by grace through personal faith. While that *can be linked with a strong family worship,* as was the case with the Puritans and other early colonists, unfortunately this was not generally done at that time.[3]

Another influence that affected the family worship was the growth of the Sunday school movement, which became an easy substitute for the father's leadership. The Sunday school movement came in because home education began to weaken in the 19th century, but when this later became church-centered education it allowed the men to rationalize that their teaching was no longer needed. While the Sunday school can be a helpful auxiliary to Christian teaching in the home, it often replaced it.

However, *the most dominant cause* for the decline of home teaching, the breakup of the family, and the loss of the sense of a national civil religion was the fact that the *men of America became almost completely preoccupied with money-making and building* a great industrial culture. This was in progress in the early 1800's and had reached explosive proportions by the time of the Civil War in the middle of the century. This led to an influx of secular philosophy which promised material progress and which began to control the educational thought. From the Civil War to the mid-twentieth century, America's commitment to obedience to Christian truth in daily life has progressively diminished. The last national day of fasting and prayer was under Andrew Johnson in the crisis Civil War days.

Man's Worship of Mammon and Sexual Infidelity

While America previously developed rapidly, it was in the first half of the 19th century that business and industry expanded at an explosive rate. Until the war with England in 1812, the United States exported goods but was dependent on English industrial production. She was also subject to English trade agreements. But after the 1812 victory, development was rapid.

For example, the yearly output of coal was 15,000 tons in 1820, 7 million tons by 1850, and 33 million by 1870. The first quarter of the century was called "the turnpike era" because so many roads were built. The construction of the Erie Canal and the National Pike further south led to widespread development of roads and canals and river transportation. The nation developed its textile industry and the iron mills. The first United States banks, as well as the first state banks, with new forms of money, bills of exchange, and means of credit, began early in the century. The steam engine, the cotton gin, the sewing machine, the mills for spinning thread and weaving, the railroad, railroad train, the telegraph, and many other machines were invented and developed.

Perhaps never in the history of the world have so many men thrown themselves into such hot pursuit of business and wealth as did the Americans. Many European magazines and books record their awe at the fact that Americans were always going to business.

Many men who were leaders in this competitive effort to gain wealth oppressed the lower classes and accepted the slavery of other men as a means of gaining wealth. While slavery existed in most of the colonies from the earliest days, in that time the chains were more on white and red men than on blacks. But black slaves became the cancer of the white southern men's greed, because they were able to work in the southern heat to grow cotton to ship to the textile mills in England, and later for mills in America.

By 1808 half of the population of Virginia was black slaves and in the Carolinas there were two for every white man. Most states had passed laws against abuses of slavery, and in 1808 the Constitution gave Congress the power to forbid importing slaves. But the cruel trade continued. The invention of the cotton gin by Eli Whitney only spread the disease more rapidly. By the time of emancipation there were four million slaves.

While I agree that slavery merited all the indignation it has aroused, unfortunately it has been depicted even worse than it was, and this has unjustifiably fanned the flames of racial bitterness.[4] The *real problem* is *individual selfish greed,* and that can be a problem for black as well as white men. Selfishness dwells in the heart of every person of every color and is the real enemy.

While the white man's greed in the South led to slavery, the greed of the northern men was bringing about equal injustices in the factories by oppressing the lower classes, including women and children. Often these were foreign immigrants whose need for work made them vulnerable. These poor people lived and worked in cramped quarters and an unhealthy environment for long hours and for meager pay. It was not until after labor unions began to gain power after the Civil War that there was any relief from such inhumane treatment.[5]

Not only did men begin to forsake and neglect their wives to make money, but they began to be involved in immorality with the lower class women. The scandal of white men in the South with the black slave women is only equaled by the less-talked-about immorality of the northern men with the women working in the factories. Prostitution began to be prevalent and male drunkenness became a conspicuous problem.

The Civil War was a divine warning to the nation. The South was left severely crippled, while the North moved ahead without much hindrance. The nation soon moved on in its rapid business and industrial expansion. From coal it went to oil, then electric power, then gasoline. It went from the Bessemer method of making steel to the open-hearth method. All of the new energy sources were accompanied by inventions such as electric lights, the radio, the automobile, and the airplane.

In the last part of the nineteenth and early twentieth centuries wealth was piled up so that there emerged the great tycoons: J. Pierpoint Morgan, the Rockefellers, et al. Male individualism reached a peak of glory as many men achieved great wealth and built large industrial and business empires.

The tremendous growth of wealth generally affected the spiritual life of the country. Wealthy men were elected to places of leadership in the churches and to the boards of trustees of the colleges, bringing with them belief in material progress, which exalted man and the things of this world rather than God and eternal values. Their influence formed the climate for the development and acceptance of anti-supernatural theology. While it had good results, especially in donations for missions, etc., money had a secularizing influence on religion itself. William Warren Sweet says, "The most significant single influence in organized religion in the United States from about the year 1880 to the end of the century and beyond, was the tremendous increase in wealth in the nation."[6]

The nation moved on in its hot pursuit of wealth only to face new tragedies—the First World War, the great depression of 1929 and following, and the Second World War. After each the pursuit of material wealth was resumed. The Second World War was followed by a new or second wave of intense mammon worship, with new technology, nuclear energy, television, computers, etc. There were new problems, with the Korean War, Vietnam, and the minority and student revolts of the 1960's. Even though most of the great tragedies primarily struck in the areas of male activities and should have been a warning to men, there was little recognized sense of divine judgment or evidence of repentance except among the young and uninfluential, such as the Jesus people.

The Resultant Changes in Woman's Role

The Early Women's Movement

Women did not always have restricted roles in America. Midge Yearley, writing on "Early American Women," said, "Women taking important roles in business, politics, the army, the ministry and the arts is not a recent phenomenon. During the colonial period, the Revolution, and the early years of our nation, women were also active in these fields. Businesses were centered in the home or in nearby offices, and women and children as well as the men worked to make a success of the family business. It was not until the 19th century when most occupations became unsuitable for women."[7]

Women began to experience bitter hurt as the men lost themselves to mammon. Wives often found themselves alone much of the time and involved in social activities that brought no monetary return. Many husbands were pursuing the dollar and neglected their wives sexually or were involved with women slaves or factory workers. Many men no longer communicated with their wives about themselves, the children, or their business, which denied recognition of them as being equal rational beings. Conflict went along with drunkenness and brutality. The women had no vote or legal recourse.

The early women's movement got started more as a social reform movement, because this was about the only acceptable way in which women could find expression. They focused on anti-slave, temperance and prostitution reforms, although the women brought in the case for their own rights and freedom as often and as boldly as they dared. In the early 1800's women's clubs began to form in America, and the first Women's Rights Congress was held in Seneca Falls, New York, July 19, 1848. At that convention the women patterned their statements after the Declaration of Independence, "We hold these truths to be self-evident: that all men *and women* are created equal, that they are endowed by their Creator with certain inalienable rights."[8]

Mrs. William D. Sporborg, in a lecture on "Women as a Social Force," traces the movement as "stirring"—1833 through 1866; "moving"—1866 to 1900; and "marching"—1900 to 1933.[9] The movement was aided by the invention of the vulcanization of rubber in the early 1800's and the application of this to mechanisms for birth control. It was also aided by the invention of the baby bottle in 1841 and also the invention of refrigeration and stoves. This released women from the necessity of nursing babies.

During the "marching" years many women indeed swung very harshly toward maleness and denied almost every difference between them and men. This was reflected in the "Chanel look" in fashion that became prominent about 1926 and 1927. Women sought to dress with a figure of a boy, even to the extent of hiding their hips and flattening their breasts.

Early Evidence Feminism Was Transgressing Nature

The women's movement then began to lose its momentum. There was no doubt a reaction to the extreme manliness of these women. Women received the right to vote in 1919, and since laws were passed that seemed to remove obstacles restricting women's rights to material gain, some women relaxed, feeling they had won much of the battle. The great economic depression hit, dimming the glory of the achievements of the men and forcing men and women to cooperate in order to survive. Also, the psychological movement came into full bloom, emphasizing the importance of sex for pleasure for women as well as men but revealing tremendous frustration and frigidity in women. Famous women psychiatrists, such as Dr. Marynia Farnham and more recently Dr. Marie Robinson, argued strongly that for women to try to be like men was sexual suicide.

About mid-century *Life* magazine interviewed eight of the most outstanding American psychiatrists as to the cause of divorce and the consensus conclusion was, "Wives are not feminine enough and husbands are not truly male." They considered that the elemental facts were, "Men are designed by nature to sire children and women to bear them."[10] Cleo Dawson, research psychologist, concluded for the National Management Association, "The supervision of women by men seems to be nature's plan, however desperately women may fight it."[11] Soon after, *Look* magazine's "New Depth Study for the American Woman," scientifically carried out by Dr. George Gallup, said that for a happy marriage situation, "the man must be the leader; he cannot be subservient to the female. Women who ask for equality with men are fighting nature."[12] McGill University studies and others backed these findings. So Margaret Mead and the women's leaders in general all fell in line and were less insistent that women leave the role of being housewives and mothers. While Dr. Mead did not give up the women's cause, she modified her views to agree with the data she found anthropologically and psychologically. Marriage stabilized and the divorce rate declined.

The tendency of women to submit is seen in the fact that some of the most ardent feminists have ended up stooping lower to men than many others. Mary Wollstonecraft, whose *A Vindication of the Rights of Women* was the initiating document for the women's movement, bowed to the whims of Gilbert Imlay as mistress and later to William Goodwin;[13] and Margaret Fuller, probably the first effective women's rights speaker in America, fell in love with an Italian, Osle, and essentially made him her god.[14]

The findings of the psychological movement have been reinforced by other careful studies, some of which were referred to in Chapter Three. Seymour Fisher, at the University of Syracuse Medical School, showed that the only psychological variable determining a woman's ability to have frequent orgasms was whether she had a male image from her father that was one of a strict standard of behavior lovingly enforced.[15] Thus a woman seems to need to think of a man as one who is a faithful leader who can be depended upon, probably because she must be dependent when having children. Shere Hite, in *The Hite Report,* which was subsidized by the National Organization for Women, takes a statement in Fisher's epilogue and twists it to claim that if women compete with men and become financially independent, this problem of orgasm will be solved.[16] It seems obvious that this is in clear conflict with his main findings.

But the psychological movement and those who called women back to their feminine role at mid-century did not solve women's problems of the loss of value, small reward for productive work, and unfulfilling routine, which we will examine in more detail. Moreover, the post-World War II achievements of men, such as nuclear power, space conquest, and the like, were more glorious than any before. Women again felt sharply the pain of neglect and a lesser value, and they now had the added pain of guilt if they did not stick to the role that psychologists had demonstrated was of their nature.

In 1963 Betty Friedan, in her book *The Feminine Mystique,* reviewed the unhappy condition of women and called for women to reject the findings of the psychologists and Margaret Mead and to charge headlong into the male domain and compete with men everywhere.[17] Kate Millett, in her book *Sexual Politics,* called for an all-out political battle for equalization.[18]

The second wave of the feminist revolution was thus

put into motion, with numerous women's organizations being formed to promote it, most prominent of which is the National Organization for Women. New birth control methods had been developed, especially the invention of the pill in 1954, which had been proven reliable in time to aid the new feminist efforts.

The Unhappy Conditions Causing the Second Wave of Feminism

The second wave of the feminist movement has been more unrestrained and intense than the beginning one. Tremendous changes had taken place in the home in the 150 years since the war with England. Women were and are hurting deeply, and their attack is now head-on.

Almost all productive labor which had material value has been removed from the home. Clothing, soap, canned goods, and other things that once were prepared at home are now bought. Jobs around the home, such as doing the laundry and washing dishes, have been made easy by machines. All this makes things easier for women at home, but it also eliminates much meaningful labor.

Public schools are taking a greater role in educating and supervising children. Mothers often are expected to help with school activities in which they have little or no creative involvement. Material values have been replacing those of character-building and moral development, so that childrearing has lost much of its significance.

School and television eat away at the time a mother can spend with her child. One study found that the average viewing time for children six to sixteen years old was twenty-two hours a week, and that by the time a child is sixteen he has watched 12,000 to 16,000 hours of television, which is almost equivalent to his learning time in school.[19] More current studies (1979) indicate it is more than this. Television now involves one-third of all men, women and children nightly. An average of twenty-nine hours per week is spent watching television by each person. Children often spend much more time than this. T.V. has become a major babysitting and child entertainment service for women. At the same time it greatly reduces communications between all members of the family.

According to Ben Stein and Jim Walters, the writers and producers of motion pictures and television programs, which are shaping the thoughts of Americans, especially children and youth, consist of only a few hundred people, most of whom hold almost the same point of view. Most of them are of a Marxist or socialist persuasion and propagate the idea that government is inefficient and bad, businessmen are evil, free love and homosexuality are good, life-long monogamous marriage is passe, military men are irrelevant or bad, murder and other crimes are most often committed by well-to-do white persons, et al. Some of the present young leaders were members of the radical Students for a Democratic Society of the 1960's, which advocated destruction of the present establishment. Their so-called documentaries on history and current events often have strategic perversions of the facts.[20] One hesitates to mention such things lest he be accused of McCarthyism. But today it may be that this very thing has caused the pendulum to swing too far, so we have lost our alertness to the dangers of Communism.

Child labor laws and public sentiment limited the opportunities for parents to teach their children by working with them and having them try their hands at creative tasks. The increased minimum wage has eliminated many jobs for young people. Thus children have been more and more separated from adults and with their peers.

As a result of all this, women found themselves doing less meaningful routine tasks that failed to challenge either their skills or their mind. Rather than being productive, they were a financial liability in a man's world that put great emphasis on material wealth.

In recent years even the noble role of bearing and nursing children has been presented negatively. With more women living through the childbearing years because of the progress of modern medicine, statisticians have warned of doom that will come through a population explosion. So today many teach that it can be morally wrong to have children. Therefore the glory of motherhood has fallen into disrepute for some.

As the purpose of sex for having children was devalued in the early twentieth century, sex for pleasure was given exaggerated emphasis. This led to the exaltation of the female body in motion pictures and in advertising. Greedy businessmen quickly seized sex as a sales gimmick, further exaggerating sex for pleasure. Women were less and less valued as whole persons and more valued as sex objects.

While the woman's role has become less important, the man's has zoomed to greater brilliance. Cobblestone streets and dusty roads have become networks of railroads, freeways, concrete malls and asphalt parking lots. Crude houses and log cabins have given way to skyscrapers and attractive subdivisions. And every new accomplishment of man is known all over the world instantly by telephone and television, often by satellite. We even had a ringside view when the first men landed on the moon. Outer space is penetrated by the listening ears of radio telescopes, and inner space is probed by electronic microscopes. All this is analyzed and recorded by complicated computers. While man has essentially built a tower to reach heaven, he has unwittingly locked his housewife counterpart into a closet, giving her little to do. But worse, he ceased to talk to her, to recognize her worth and the worth of her job—failing to treat her as his equal.

Margaret Mead once said, "We have been suffering

from an undervaluation of the woman's role and an over-valuation of the man's role." Mrs. Mead further tells us that in a primitive tribe having and nurturing babies "is a very conspicuous act when the largest thing a man builds is a house twenty feet high."[21] But on the awesome stage of modern male culture, the job of producing and caring for a human life is deceptively dwarfed. Moreover, a woman is applauded only a moment for having a baby, while man's achievements are continually before us.

A man can move up from his job to one of more respon-sibility, and with each move he gets more money and recognition. But when a housewife has a baby it costs money and gives her little status in the world. This can cause women to feel a painful lack of identity and worth and to become bored, with just cause for their revolt. But a person in pain is prone to ignore other important factors than those which seem to give immediate relief. I believe the feminist advocates are ignoring important facts in their efforts to remove this pain. They now want to *be like men,* not just be counted of equal value. Obvious differences are being ignored.

Feminist Architects Aim to Destroy Marriage and Establish Matriarchy

Most of the designers and captains of the feminist move-ment have been women who have suffered abuse from men and have been driven by hate. Dr. Marynia Farnham described the movement as she observed it 100 years after the first women's congress, "The real goal of the feminist movement was to eradicate men. A document more against men you cannot imagine than that formulated by the American feminists when they first met in 1848. They [since] demanded the instant abolition of marriage as a form of slavery for women. They demanded the institution of uterine descent, namely, no child to be named for its father, but always for its mother. The mother was to dictate the nature of the union and the disposition of the child. I have seen recent documents demanding that men be ousted from all public office except engineering, and that women take over the control of all party politics."[22] Speaking of the radical feminists of the second wave, *Time* magazine said, "Their eschatological aim is to topple the patriarchal system in which men by birthright control all of society's levers of power—in government, industry, education, science, the arts."[23]

As has been pointed out, the first wave of feminism began in the second quarter of the nineteenth century and the second wave began in the 1960's. They followed two of the periods when American men were forsaking their wives for wealth and achievement. We have argued that this distortion of the male role creates a painful condition for women and leads to men further distorting their role and the role of the women (see pp. 43–47).

Abuse by and hate of men was characteristic also of the earlier European feminists such as Mary Wollstonecraft, her daughter Mary Shelley (who wrote Frankenstein), Mary's friend Frances Wright, George Sand, and others. The abuse and hate in the lives of Lucy Stone, Elizabeth Cady Stanton, Sarah M. Grimke, and other early American feminists is also clear.

As was previously pointed out, the painful condition of women resulted from the male addiction to mammon worship and their consequent immorality. In seeking relief, the women followed the lead of the men and began to fight to gain the same values that their errant men had established. They launched a fight to get all the freedoms for status and wealth, and often for immorality, which their husbands were indulging in. In order to achieve these, their chief objective was to remove all male supremacy, and to do that they saw the removal of marriage restraints as pivotal to their success. The efforts to call men back to putting God first, with obedience to Him in loving care and faithfulness to their wives and children, were only weakly pursued. The feminists mainly chose rather to catch the disease of pursuing wealth which the men had and kill the body (of marriage) rather than cure the patient of the disease.

From the earliest days of the American feminist movement the removal of the marriage bond was considered by its key designers as essential to obtaining their freedom. Elizabeth Cady Stanton was the woman at the first Women's Rights Congress who first interpreted constitutional equality for women in terms of doing what men do. While she wanted freedom within marriage, she wanted easy divorce. She wrote to Susan B. Anthony in 1853, advocating promotion of divorce, and said, "I feel, as never before, that this whole question of women's rights *turns on the pivot of the marriage relation. . . .*" Again to Anthony in 1860 she wrote, "How this marriage question grows on me. It *lies at the foundation* of all progress" (italics mine). But she herself was not willing to openly attack the subject because she felt the world was not ready.

The aim of the early feminists was not primarily at the male abuses of marriage, but at marriage itself. The desire of these women to remove male leadership from the home was *not* the view of most American women. Henry Blackwell, who willingly signed a paper giving up male leadership privileges to marry Lucy Stone (who kept her own name and separate domicile), said, "I believe nineteen women out of twenty would be unhappy with a husband who, like myself, would repudiate supremacy."[24]

The hard-core extreme feminists of today are clearly continuing to aim at the dissolution of the family, although they have no clear alternative. They see more clearly than the moderates that removal of the male role in the family is the only way to achieve their objectives.

Some are aiming at the goal of dissolution of the family by 2000 A.D. Such leaders as Ti-Grace Atkinson, former leader of National Organization for Women, Kate Millett, and others are insistent on destroying the family. Kate Millet, whose book *Sexual Politics* became the handbook for the feminist revolution, says that the family is patriarchy's chief institution and cell for sexist brainwashing, which not only encourages its own members to adjust and conform, but acts as a unit in the patriarchal state which rules its citizens through the family heads. She admits that an end to patriarchy will probably destroy the family.

Three Categories of Feminist Advocates

The feminist advocates today fall into three main categories: (1) those who are the main *hard-core architects* who have been hurt by men and/or involved in lust and greed, (2) those who are well-intending do-gooders and want to *promote personal human rights,* and (3) those who feel that New Testament *biblical Christian truth teaches* that because women also equally receive the Holy Spirit there should be no distinction between the roles of men and women. The last two groups include men and women.

The last group will be considered in the next section of this book. The second group, the human rights advocates, are often reputable people who are greatly influenced by the hard-core leaders to see the wrong done to individuals and to support them in their fight. However, they do not see the long-range effects on the family and on society, nor do they consider that other solutions might give more freedom and satisfaction for all individuals. These people are very earnest and self-righteous about this cause and can't see why anyone could be so insensitive to *individual* human need as to be against the movement.

Radical hard-core feminists are the real leaders of the other two groups. The hard-core leaders of the feminist movement today do not hold the views of the average American woman. Examples of some of them follow. Midge Costanza, one-time aide to President Carter, has said in regard to homosexuality, "I get very emotional about this issue because I feel very strongly that you should have the right to love whomever you want. *I do.*" Gloria Steinem, editor of *Ms* magazine, has said, "The overthrow of capitalism should accompany the overthrow of the institution of marriage." She also wrote, "By the year 2000 we will, I hope, raise our children to believe in human potential, not God."[25] Bella Abzug, New York congresswoman, chairperson of the Commission of the International Women's Year that held the 1977 women's conference in Houston, Texas, and former chairperson of the President's advisory committee on women, introduced a "civil rights" bill for homosexuals. Jean O'Leary, a former nun but now coexecutive director of the National Gay Task Force and an appointee to the President's Commission on Observance of I. W. Y., advocates studies in our schools to help our children accept the idea of homosexuality as an alternate life style. Eleanor Smeal, head of the National Organization for Women, became interested in feminism because of her frustrating confinement after the birth of a child and now advocates government nurseries for children into which a child *must* be put at two years of age in order to free the mother. Kate Millett's recent autobiographically based book airs her psychological problems that resulted from a lengthy affair with a dominating lesbian.[23] Betty Friedan, the "mother" of the current wave of feminism, has said that their objective is to restructure all of society. At the I. W. Y. meeting in Houston she announced she is now willing to include the fight for lesbian rights in the women's movement.

Marriage and Sexual Perversion

Homosexuality is Socially Destructive

Homosexuality is the end of responsible society, and promoting homosexual rights is now prominent in the ERA goals. Each individual homosexual looks after self-interest and self pleasure. While there are some so-called homosexual "marriages," most of those that last even for a few years tend to be turbulent and are usually marked by unfaithfulness. If homosexual marriages endured and all men and women adopted this, no children would result, and society would die in one generation. It is a principle that cannot be universally applied and inclines toward death. It represents the ultimate in exalting the individual over social order. Homosexuality as a universal model is suicidal for society. (See pp. 128–131 for further discussion on homosexuality.)

However, it is a misconception to think that homosexuals are all peculiar people. Many are very capable and not distinguishable from straight heterosexuals. Many of these act both homosexually and heterosexually, calling themselves bisexual. But their *homosexual activity* is *socially destructive.*

Stable Marriage is Basic for Society

It has often been said, "Marriage is the germ cell of society." From marriage come our religious, civil, and other forms of government for human relationships. Hence, promiscuous forms of heterosexual acts are also socially destructive. The most basic social responsibility is fidelity in marriage. When one is dishonest in marriage, truthfulness has been destroyed in the most intimate relationship, and dishonesty will develop in other relationships.

Dr. David Reuben, author of *Everything You Always Wanted to Know about Sex—But Were Afraid to Ask,* can hardly be accused of defending restricting concepts of sex-for-pleasure. He has said, "A nuclear family consists of father, mother, and children standing alone against all adversity. In effect, it is the kind of arrangement that human beings have instinctively chosen for the last 50,000 years. From the steaming jungles of Africa to the frozen polar wastelands, Mommy, Daddy, and Baby have stood united against the threats of Nature and civilization. Over and over, the cultures with the strongest family ties—both social and emotional—have produced the best-adapted and most mature adults. But now social innovators have what they think are better ideas." After reviewing the ideas of "trial" marriage, "group" marriage, and "renewable" marriage, he said, "They work just fine—in the daydreams of those who think them up. When they are tried out with real people, the results are almost uniformly disappointing."[27]

Margaret Mead affirms this anthropological truth. She has said, "Over and over again, throughout history, there have been attempts to destroy this family unit and to invoke mythological past happenings to justify contemporary social experiments, such as the assertion that in earlier times there was no family and human beings practiced 'group marriage,' for example. So far in human history, however, societies have not found a way to rear children without the ties of parents to children and children to parents."[28]

Sorokin has said, "Marriage has been regarded by all societies as the culminating point of human existence, and as the most decisive factor in the survival and well-being of the societies themselves."[29]

It is time to face historical reality: if marriage and the family go, then society will go with them. Why should we commit social suicide by following sexual radicals?

While the distortion of roles is not the only cause of the disintegration of society, it seems obvious that distortions, abuses, and irresponsibility as to roles in the family *are the chief cause.* If this continues to occur there will be an increasing frustration of husbands, wives, and children. Families will continue to disintegrate, be unhappy, and promote further sexual promiscuity, frustration, hate and escapism. These hates and distortions will be passed to successive offspring, "visiting the iniquities of the fathers upon the children to the third and fourth generations" (Exodus 20:5,6).

Stable Marriage and Sexual Pleasure

The issue of sex for pleasure desperately needs to be reevaluated. We have had our studies by Kinsey, David Reuben, Masters and Johnson and many others. The latest is that of Masters and Johnson in which they proclaim that homosexuals have greater pleasure in sex than do most heterosexuals. They say the homosexuals are less inhibited and have developed better foreplay techniques for sex pleasure.[30]

There are two main questions that expose the fallacy of the emphasis of all these studies. This latest by Masters and Johnson shows the weakness more than any other. The first question is, is sex pleasure so important for genuine happiness that it should be given prominence over all else in life? The second is, is laboratory evaluation of sex for pleasure an adequate way to evaluate attainment of sex pleasure for everyone? There is considerable evidence that both questions must be answered *No!* If that be true, then the great masses of American people have been deceived and led astray.

First, let it be said that many of the findings of various sex studies can have some beneficial results if combined with a proper value system and with an understanding of responsible relationships. But most (not all) of these studies have been used in such a way as to destroy proper values and responsible relationships. Ironically enough, because this is true I am convinced they have actually been destructive of the attainment of sexual pleasure for many.

Sex pleasure alone is not the most important thing for genuine happiness. Those who have pursued sexual pleasure as a priority, spending more time studying and pursuing this, have a much higher incidence of psychological disorders than do people committed to life-long monogamy. This is true whether they be heterosexuals or homosexuals. I know of no study that evaluates this, but many years of counseling experience and my acquaintance with counseling therapy through the years has revealed an overwhelming conviction that this is true. Men and women who have had the most affairs and sought sex pleasure the most often have the deepest psychological problems. Also, the older they get the deeper those problems become.

When sex is pursued for selfish pleasure it loses its meaning. Dr. Franz Winkler, an eminent psychiatrist, has said, "The real problem with sex relations today is that it frequently becomes a mutual form of self-satisfaction, in which each partner thinks more or less of himself, women more than men. The moment this exists all real sex experience disappears. It becomes masturbation."[31]

Moreover, while people who are sexually immoral heterosexually, homosexually, or in other ways (bestiality, etc.) may live functionally productive lives, the rate of genuine creative productivity is much lower for them than for those who give sex pleasure a more moderate emphasis or who abstain sexually.[32] As one grows older, he or she begins to feel life has been useless. Having attained so many orgasms does not give a person a sense of value. But also important is the fact that others in society have received little of beneficial lasting help from the sensually oriented life.

The laboratory analysis of sex does not give a good evaluation of how to achieve maximum sex pleasure in life situations and over the long run. It primarily evaluates degrees of sex pleasure with a partner under an observed situation for the moment. My experience in marriage counseling indicates that maximum pleasure in sex over the long period comes when there is a feeling of maximum trust of the partner and a feeling that the other person cares for them. This is more obvious for women than for men, but is true for both. When there are feelings of hostility toward the partner, ability to respond decreases greatly. Selfishness and competitiveness therefore greatly hinder sex pleasure. A woman cannot physically respond if she has developed hostilities against men, from her home or later experiences.[33] I have had cases where hate has so restricted the woman that penetration was mechanically impossible until hostility against males was removed by counseling. I have had cases where men become impotent and thought their sex life ended until they found release from hostilities. Distrust can reduce response in direct proportion.

Therefore a person who selfishly pursues sex pleasure soon creates hostilities in the partner and therefore soon finds that partner less desirable. Hence, he or she searches for another partner who does not feel hate. Promiscuity then becomes a pattern. When sexual performance is analyzed in a laboratory the two partners approach sex more from an indifferent point of view without those hostilities. But if the partners are those who must establish long-range relationships without corrective counseling, the performance will be affected.

Moreover, most people, especially women, cannot completely release themselves to the partner and enjoy themselves unless the sex act is private. This is especially true of those who hold that the sex act should be an intimate and sacred expression of complete self-giving to that one and only person. Many women cannot release themselves even if they are alone with their partner behind locked doors if children or someone else *might* overhear the activity. Yet these same women may repeatedly achieve exciting orgasms under more confidential conditions.

Therefore, laboratory analysis of sex pleasure is not a test for sexual pleasure for those who see its importance to responsible intimate relationships, but only for those who have rejected that interpretation of sex. Homosexuals generally have hostilities toward the opposite sex, and do not see it as a means of bearing common children and of building a socially responsible family. If they have come to the point of willingness to make this known, they are most free to perform sexually before others because they are already hardened to observing opinions. Hence, the results of Masters and Johnson are not a good test of comparison to heterosexual responses.

Soon after I wrote this, Ann Landers devoted her column to this subject and expressed views that agree. She said, "Regarding Masters and Johnson's findings: It should be remembered that laboratory sex is very different from bedroom sex. When I first read of their earlier work, I had serious questions about the 'normalcy' of couples who would have sexual intercourse under klieg lights, while being photographed and monitored, not to mention the encumbrances of intrauterine cameras, tape recorders, devices to record blood pressure, muscle tension, and lubrication. There has been much controversy among many psychiatrists about Masters and Johnson's statement, 'Both homosexuality and heterosexuality are learned responses'."[34]

Those who have most fully died to their own self-interest and submitted their wills to God to obey Him and care for others are the persons who repeatedly over the long run have the maximum pleasure in sex. Christianity teaches that one should go to the marriage bed first to give pleasure to his or her partner and secondarily to gain pleasure for self. As a result both partners receive the most possible pleasure. "It is more blessed to give than to receive" (Acts 20:35). The biblical instruction is for a marriage partner to make his or her body available for the spouse's benefit (1 Corinthians 7:3–5). Such attitudes promote trust of the other person and allow maximum response.

Redbook magazine carried out perhaps the most extensive survey ever done of women's sexual responses. One hundred thousand women answered their sex questions. The results were contrary to the popularized view that religious people are restrained, forbidding, and unsatisfied with sex. The *Redbook* report said, *"Sexual satisfaction is related significantly to religious belief.* With notable consistency, the greater the intensity of a woman's religious convictions, the likelier she is to be highly satisfied with the sexual pleasures of marriage. . . . The women who describe themselves on the questionnaire as 'strongly religious' are more likely to be satisfied with their sex lives than women who describe themselves as 'fairly religious' or 'mildly religious'. . . . Moderately religious wives, in turn, are more likely to be satisfied than women who describe themselves as 'not religious.' This tendency exists among women of all ages." It was found that this was not related to frequency of sex because there was no significant difference in frequency. Moreover, religious wives seemed more satisfied than the non-religious with the frequency.[35]

This data should be combined with that of Seymour Fisher at Syracuse University which showed that the women most regularly reaching orgasm were those who had an image of their father as a person who had high moral standards that were firmly and kindly enforced.

They apparently had an image of men as people they could trust.[36] Very probably the religious factor (as shown by the *Redbook* survey, but not demonstrated by Fisher) contributed the idea of trust that also allowed self-giving. All of this would lead one to conclude that a partner who endorses sexual promiscuity would *in the long run* be the least satisfying. This would also mean that many authorities on sex have really been leading millions of Americans down the wrong road. The Playboy philosophy or that of the feminist who advocates sexual freedom for women without marriage are misguided, and are destroying meaningful sex for thousands of people.

The most recent research in regard to sexual problems was conducted by Dr. Harold I. Lief, director of the Marriage Council of Philadelphia, and by Dr. Helen Singer Kaplan, head of the human sexuality program at New York Hospital-Cornell Medical Center. They found that the No. 1 complaint by people with sexual problems was the loss of sexual desire, and in fifty percent of these cases this was caused by the breakdown of the personal relationship between the couple. This major problem was bypassed by Masters and Johnson, who focused on the mechanics of the sex act. If more and more people don't want to play in the game, what good are instructions on *how* to play the game? Moreover, this recent research showed that it is much easier to correct by counseling the functions of sex (60 to 80% cure) than it is to change those with lost motivation (10% cure).[37]

If we are to restore greater sexual pleasure to life, it seems that the answer is to bring men and women back to a commitment to God and to life-long monogamous marriage. When a man and woman commit themselves to each other for life, and a partner is not seen as disposable for the slightest dislike, then the maximum trust and unselfishness becomes possible. Sexual fidelity *can* cause greater sexual pleasure.

Conclusion

United States history reveals all the elements that make for the breakdown of the family. Faith in God has been taken lightly, and the selfishness of men and women has destroyed sexual balance. First, the men, generally speaking, began to turn away from the worship of God to the pursuit of material wealth. For many this led to loss of relationships with their wives and children and to the pursuit of sex for pleasure in immoral relationships. This occurred in two major waves. The first was in the first half of the nineteenth century and the second about the middle of the twentieth century.

Secondly, many women revolted because of their neglect and loss of value, and demanded to be like men in access to material gain and sexual freedom for pleasure. The first wave of feminism reached strong expression about mid-nineteenth century and the second about 1960 and following. As a result, children have been increasingly unwanted and neglected. Women are fast turning their backs on the home for money and success outside.

While the wealth of the American home has grown to amazing amounts, the family has begun to suffer from the conflict between the sexes. Sex for begetting children has radically diminished, and sex for pleasure, heterosexual or homosexual, seems to dominate. Meaningful relationships among people are disintegrating toward anarchy. The individual and his or her rights have become of primary importance over society.

Chapter 5

THE PATTERN OF ROLE CHANGING IN HISTORY AND THE DECLINE OF SOCIETY

Importance of Historical Pattern

In Chapter Three we looked at the similarities and differences of men and women and evaluated the ways men and women can fail in their roles and thereby destroy each other's sexual identity. We showed evidence that distortion of roles causes loss of interdependence and the glue for society. In Chapter Four we have seen how this has actually been happening in the United States. The man in his idolatrous pursuit of material wealth and status through achievement has so overexaggerated his role that women have rebelled against the feminine role, to become like men and eradicate man's power. We tried to trace through American history the pattern it has taken. In Chapter Six we will look at the ill effects of selfish individualism on American life.

It now is important to see if such a pattern has been frequent in history. In a longer and more detailed book on the pattern of decline of society in history, I intend to examine this in detail. But here it is important to explore briefly the pattern of social decline in two societies which are relevant to this book. The value of this is two-fold. One, if the pattern has commonly occurred before, then it confirms our analysis of what is happening in America. Secondly, if the primary cause of the pattern of decline can be further documented, it may then be possible to advocate a way to remove the cause and bring renewal.

Misconception about Status of Women

It is commonly held by the feminists that women have emerged from a caveman situation in which they were subdued and dominated by men and that woman is now evolving toward her freedom for the first time. This assumption about the history of women has been shown to be incorrect. In fact, Charles Seltman of Cambridge University, in his book *Women in Antiquity,*[1] has argued that women in ancient times enjoyed far greater liberty than modern women. He then tried to attribute domination of the man over the woman in modern times to the Apostle Paul. We will present evidence that the early rabbis considered Paul one of the liberals of his day and that Jewish rabbinical leaders in Palestine had reacted to the feminist movements that had taken place in ancient Greece and Rome and had taken an extremely conservative position, restricting women's rights severely. Seltman shows the great freedom that women enjoyed in antiquity, but he misses the fact that the status of women actually changed as society went through a process of degeneration.

The Steps of Decline in Ancient Greece

Greek men began to turn *from a spiritual* to a mechanical view of life and toward materialism in the sixth century B.C. Their very early respect for God as a higher governing intelligence already had naturalistic attachments by historical times, but the high respect for Zeus so evident in early history gradually disintegrated into skepticism and a pluralism of gods and goddesses that were more anthropomorphic and sensual. Plato, Aristotle, and Anaxagoras reflect later on the fact that the Greeks once held to a governing intelligence as the beginning of all things, and Pythagoras, Xenophanes, Empedocles, and Democritus assailed the myths and held to a higher religion.

The Greek nation turned strongly *toward materialism* and the men began to forsake their wives in the pursuit of wealth following the time of the Cleisthenes democracy (510 B.C. ff). This was the time of developing shipping, mining silver in Athens, centralizing government and taxing the surrounding areas. The treasury was developed, with banking in the Acropolis, and there was an explosion of education. Materialism reached great heights during the time of Pericles. Euripides commented on the painful conditions of women in the early fifth century (cf. his play *Medea, 213–251*). They were under severe restrictions and their men were occupied by commerce, war and wealth. There existed a double standard in morality, and homosexuality increased, partially from association with the Spartans in the Persian War. The Spartans had accepted it from Crete much earlier. Conditions for children worsened. Euripides said, "Child, why are you crying? Where have those smiles gone?"

A *women's revolt* was generated, and by 425 B.C. we find Plato calling for as radical a movement of women's rights as anyone in modern times. In his book on *Laws,* Chapter VII, and in *The Republic,* Book V, 449–460, he claims that there is practically no difference in men and women, and that women should do everything men do. They should go to war and fight just as the men do and should be responsible for all the things that the men are. The only difference, he said, is that they occasionally have children.

The revolt of the women reached its climax toward the end of the fifth century and is expressed in Aristophanes' plays *Lysistratae* and *Ecclesiazusae.* While no other records indicate these as exact historical events, any play critic will agree that had they no basis in historic fact, they would have offered no amusement to the viewers. A women's movement was evident in the days that followed. In the first play the women took over the Acropolis and locked the gates, insisting they handle the money and negotiate the war. When men tried to break through the gates to get the money, the women threw cold water on them and demanded their rights. In the other play women disguised themselves as men and penetrated the voting assembly to achieve their goals. The process of feminization began, and the third and second centuries became known as "the age of women." Women moved into every area of life, even presiding at the Olympic games and in one case over a synagogue.

In the century that followed Aristophanes, sexual anarchy began to take over. These were the years when Hermaphroditus and Aphrodite, the goddess of love, began to be primary. Mixed bath houses, proliferation of courtesans, acceptance of adultery and widespread prostitution followed. The temple prostitutes were multiplied by the thousands, and divorce became a common thing in ancient Greece. This led to the breakdown of the home and finally brought anarchy.

During this time the importance of the rights of the individual began to dominate over the social good. The philosophy of Aristotle rejected transcendent ideals and emphasized individual particulars in realism. Social trends had prepared the way for philosophical views that would further forward *individualism* and ultimately collective individualism (see pp. 86–88). The men emphasized their privileges and rights for the material and sensual. The women responded by demanding theirs. Gaining more "freedom," they became vulnerable and abused. Children were neglected and misused homosexually and in many other ways, leading to efforts to defend the rights of the young.

The greed of the upper classes led to a gap in living standards, which in turn lead to class wars. The Aegean Islands revolted, causing the Social War. The revolt of the Phocians brought on the Sacred War. Then the colonies revolted, one after another, because Athens had taken economic advantage of them. With the growth of this *anarchy* the glory of Greece came to an end. This led to the dictatorship of Philip II of Macedon, the father of Alexander the Great.

The Steps of Decline in the Roman Republic

The Roman Republic went through a similar process, turning to materialism very strongly in about 241 B.C., after the first Punic War. The *worship of a single spirit* (known by this time as Jupiter) *was replaced* by a more naturalistic, sensual, and finally more pluralistic type of worship.

The conquests of the Romans *expanded wealth* by the seizing of land and by the taxation of the people they had conquered. The development of a merchant fleet, governmental control through their brilliant code of laws, and military policing of the roads and sea lanes all led to great wealth. The Romans pursued wealth with great zeal after the first Punic War. During the second Punic War laws restricting wealth for women produced friction between the women and men and finally led to a women's revolt. Valerius wrote of the women's bad conditions.

The *revolt of the women* reached a climax at the time

of Cato in 195 B.C. and is recorded by Livy. The women stormed the Roman senate, demanded certain freedoms, and refused to leave until they got what they wanted. They came in from all the villages and had what might be called a women's rights congress, demanding equal rights with men. Otto Keefer tells us that their chief motivation was access to material gain and also the ability to enjoy sex freely, as men could.[2] From that point on, the women gained the rights they wanted. In the succeeding decades the nation began to be dominated by competition between the men and women and there was tremendous growth of immorality, divorce and breakdown of the home. The law of manus, or submission to the husband, as required by the law of confarreatio, gave way to the law of usus, which removed the husband's authority and allowed easy divorce.

Prostitution was prevalent. It was later supported by the government, and the privilege to go to the prostitutes was given as a part of welfare support. Immorality and divorce prevailed.

During this period the Romans embraced the Epicurean philosophy of individual pleasure and then reacted toward the Stoic philosophy, which came to dominate the intellectual thought. The Stoics, being pantheists, had no place for transcendent ideals. They laid stress on natural law, seeing each man as an end in himself. Like Aristotle, they emphasized *the individual.* B. A. G. Fuller has said of the Stoic, "The existent is concrete and individual, and universals are merely names marking the superficial resemblances of particular things."[3]

The family became more and more disintegrated, placing greater responsibility on a Roman government that represented more and more fragmented groups. The government was pressured by the big agricultural interests and other groups. The lower class plebians revolted against the controlling wealthy class. By about 133 B.C.

there was a terrible time of anarchy and chaos in the nation. The whole peninsula finally rebelled against Rome. In the end Julius Caesar was given dictatorial power to try to quell the rampant anarchy.

Thus in Greece and Rome we observe the same pattern of spiritual failure, role distortion and breakdown of society as has occurred in America.

The Common Pattern of Decline in Many Nations

The pattern in ancient Greece, in the Roman Republic, and in America is the same:

1. Men ceased to lead their families in worship. Spiritual and moral development became secondary. Their view of God became more naturalistic, mathematical and mechanical.

2. Men selfishly neglected care of their wives and children to pursue material wealth, political and military power, and cultural development. Material values began to dominate thought, and the man began to exalt his own role as an individual.

3. Men, being preoccupied with business or war, either neglected their wives sexually or became involved with lower-class women or with homosexuality, and a double standard of morality developed.

4. The role of women at home and with children lost value and status. Women, being neglected and their roles devalued, revolted to gain access to material wealth and also freedom for sex outside marriage. Women began to minimize having sex relations to conceive children, and the emphasis became sex for pleasure. Laws regulating marriage made divorce easy.

5. Husbands and wives competed against each other for money, home leadership, and the affection of their children, resulting in hostility and frustration and possible

homosexuality in the children. Many marriages ended in separation and divorce. Many children were unwanted, aborted, abandoned, molested, and undisciplined. The more undisciplined children became, the more social pressure there was not to have children. The breakdown of the home produced anarchy.

6. Selfish individualism grew and was carried over into society, fragmenting it into smaller and smaller group loyalties. The nation was thus weakened by internal conflict. The decrease in the birthrate produced an older population that had less ability to defend itself and less will to do so, making the nation more vulnerable to its enemies.

7. As unbelief in God became more complete and parental authority diminished, ethical and moral principles disappeared, affecting the economy and government. Thus, by internal weakness and fragmentation the societies came apart. There was no way to save them except by a dictator who arose from within or invaded from without.

This *chain of events began by the men turning from God to pursue material wealth, and each successive step occurred automatically. Like dominoes,* one falls, causing the next to fall, and then the next. The first is the cause of the second, the second the third, and so on. Worship of God, abandoned for greed or idolatry, was the first to fall, and finally, when the family collapsed, there was little hope of renewal. *This is the main thesis of this book!*

This pattern has been many times repeated. J. D. Unwin, in his book *Sex and Culture,* analyzed 59 preliterate societies and some societies in history,[4] and he came to a conclusion which was sustained by Pitirim Sorokin in his book *The American Sex Revolution,* namely, that societies were able to advance to a highly rationalistic culture only when they had a spiritual patriarchal type government, maintained their sexual life within marriage, and were chaste and temperate. They inevitably declined whenever they departed from this basic pattern.[5]

In the Bible covetousness, or greed, is equated with idolatry and is said to lead to sensuous conduct (cf. worship of the golden calf, Exodus 32; Romans 1:22–27; and Colossians 3:5, where Paul says, "Greed is idolatry").

Idolatry in ancient societies always involved role distortions. Baal, Marduk, Molech, and others were gods offering material prosperity. They were succeeded by feminine goddesses representing wealth and sensuality. Ashtoreth, the Canaanite female goddess, meant "to be rich," and was the counterpart of Ishtar in Assyria and other goddesses.

The closing days of most societies were characterized by the predominance of a female deity. The goddess Ishtar conferred the ring and staff on the king of Mari prior to his conquest by Hammurabi. The eighteenth dynasty of Egypt was dominated by Hathor, the cow goddess, who protected the Pharaoh. Her power declined after God's judgment and the exodus of Israel from Egypt. Aphrodites in ancient Greece and Venus in Rome were prominent near the time of decay. The cult of Tammuz and the worship of the queen of heaven led the prophets to predict Israel's final end (see Ezekiel 8:14; Jeremiah 44:17,25).

Changes in the View of the Individual

I have pointed out above that the selfish individualism of the man elicits a selfish reaction in the woman, and these breed selfish undisciplined children. Thus, the concept of the individual seems to change as society decays, and helps effect that decay. In the beginning the individual seems to be responsible to God and for others. Gradually he becomes valuable in himself and his identity and security are based on material wealth. Selfish individualism results, which makes the state and all society a tool for the individual's rights and benefits. Such selfish individualism begins to fragment the society and ultimately destroys it. Then all individuals submit their rights to authoritarian government for their collective material benefit. Thus, selfish individualism destroys freedom and all rights. The steps of individualism may be summarized as follows:

Theistic   Steward before God: the individual is a creature of God and valuable because God made him; he is a steward, to care for God, for self and others.

Deistic   Endowed individual rights: the individual has natural value in himself and should be free to gain for self.

Democratic   Self-earned individual rights: every individual ought to have a right to equal wealth and should vote and control government so he gets what he deserves.

Collective   Government-guaranteed individual rights: the governing elite should assure each individual of equal rights to equal wealth by redistribution and control. The importance of the individual is placed above the family. Strong police control is needed to restrain selfish individualism.

Dictatorial   The individuals are the tools of the state dictator. The objective is to preserve material prosperity for the masses.

This would indicate that America is only one step away from the end. We are more and more demanding that the government distribute wealth and control all things. Aleksandr Solzhenitsyn said in his 1978 commencement address at Harvard, "The defense of individual rights has reached such extremes as to make society as a whole defenseless against certain individuals. It is time in the West to defend not so much human rights as human obligations."

Chapter 6

AMERICA AT THE BRINK OF ANARCHY AND DICTATORSHIP?

Where is the United States in the chain of events that lead to the breakdown of a society? In the second chapter it was said that the United States is reaching the crisis point as the family becomes disoriented and many break down. In this chapter we will look at the evidence that individualism is dominant over concern for others and society in general. Prevailing attitudes of men and women toward individual financial gain or pleasure and toward the family are destructive. The results to children are tragic. I believe we are moving rapidly toward anarchistic conditions economically, politically, educationally, and in civil government. The result could be dictatorship, as in other nations that have gone down this road.

Individualism Has Precedence Over Society

The focus on the *individual* and his rights *over and above the family* and other social institutions has emerged as a dominant factor in recent American history. Trends in life in western Europe and America have generated conditions conducive to a philosophy favoring the individual. The views of John Locke, F. Bacon, and Adam Smith forwarded the idea that individual material progress is the main good and that the state should exist for the individual's benefit. Immanuel Kant's philosophy, influenced by the views of Locke, Berkeley, and Hume that all knowledge comes through sense perception, argued that man was born with categories of thought but that these do not extend to the infinite. By persuasively drawing a philosophical line between the temporal and the infinite, the subsequent generations went toward interpreting all knowledge in terms of naturalism or pantheism. If there is no knowledge of eternal and heavenly things, only the natural is left to believe in.

Therefore George Hegel's pantheistic philosophy became influential on all modern thinkers, especially his emphasis on freedom and the individual. Hegel went beyond Locke in his emphasis on the individual. He said selfish individual desire is the spirit of history that evolves toward human freedom and is the work and aim of God in the world. This emphasis on selfish individualism is evident in logical positivism and also especially in existential philosophy, which places prime importance on the existence or survival of the individual. All theological and ethical thought has been affected by this philosophical thought. Charles Darwin's theory of organic evolution based on "the survival of the fittest" has also been used to vindicate selfish individualism.

As Aristotelianism, Epicureanism, and Stoicism promoted individualism and the decay of society in ancient Greece and Rome, so post-Kantian and post-Hegelian philosophies have promoted the individual instead of society in the West. In the context of the abuse of one person or group by another, it seems so right to defend offended individuals. But in a deceptive way this defense of the individual can be pushed to the point of destroying social responsibility, which in turn leads to the loss of the freedom of the individual. The rights of the individual often are best protected when his relationships to others are preserved.

Modern thought in America is focusing almost entirely on the rights of the individual over the social good. Dr. William Glasser has said, ". . . People today concern themselves more and more with an independent role—their identity." Paul Vitz speaks of "selfism" in *Psychology as Religion: The Cult of Self-Worship.*[1] Dr. Francis Schaeffer, the noted Christian apologist, has pointed out that today people are concerned only with personal peace and prosperity. Many books, Christian and secular, have focused on self-image and self-love. Recent literature has exalted individual self-interest and privilege. Robert Alberti and Michael Emmons advocate "self-assertion" in *Your Perfect Right.* Ayn Rand's books, *The Fountainhead, Atlas Shrugged,* and *For the New Intellectual,* emphasize the "ethic of rational self-interest." There are also Robert Ringer's best sellers, *Winning Through Intimidation* and *Looking Out for No. 1,* and others. A major New York publisher has begun a magazine named *Self.* Widely advertised are the "Me" books for children. Because of our self-centered and individualistic outlook, Tom Wolfe has called the 1970's "the 'Me' decade."

Unfortunately, today in the U. S. many influential people have been deceived into supporting legislation and movements which weaken the family because on the surface they seem to forward *individual* human rights. Thus, as the family decays, the freedom of the individual is suffering and an emphasis on collectivism is resulting, leading toward dictatorship.

Man's Leadership in Mammon Worship and the National Effects

Mammon Worship Distorts Sexual Roles and Threatens the Economy

The trends which began in the early nineteenth century have become like a tidal wave in recent years. The man's spiritual leadership of his home has almost disappeared in favor of gaining wealth and success. Ironically, more and more people have become associated with the churches while worship and application and obedience to God's laws have diminished at home and in personal life.

The movement toward anarchy in America is growing rapidly. By the middle of the twentieth century men had virtually abdicated their position of authority in the home in exchange for material gain. Leading Roman Catholic sociologists and marriage counselors meeting for the National Catholic Family Life Convention in Buffalo, N. Y., in July, 1958, agreed that the main reason for man's loss of authority in the home was his pursuit of material gain. The leading spokesman, Dr. A. H. Clemens of Catholic University, Washington, pointed out that the man no longer had time for anything but financial success, so the home was left to the woman. Having lost status at home, he then sought to gain it by greater material success, trapped in a vicious cycle of value seeking. Women reacted, so that by 1957 there were eight proposed constitutional amendments for women (e.g. ERA).

Shortly thereafter (ca. 1960) the second wave of the women's movement began aiming at removing every vestige of male control of society to achieve the rights of women to material gain and sexual freedom. Multitudes of women moved out into the work force to gain their share of money and financial independence. As many women have forsaken the home to gain freedom and self-sufficiency, other women have been encouraged by their husbands to leave their small children and get a job in order to help provide a higher living standard for the family.

During this period greed has led to irresponsible fiscal policies in both the private and public areas of our nation. It took 174 years (to 1962) to put the first $100 billion in the federal budget, nine years to put the second, four years to put the third, two years to put the fourth and only one year to put the fifth—that budget being now, in 1979, nearly $500 billion. It was predicted that the federal debt would be $874 billion by the end of 1979. But for a citizen to put all the blame on government would be to use it as a scapegoat. Private debt also sky-rocketed, from $37.9 billion in 1946 to $1,100 billion in 1978. In 1967 the money supply (currency, checkbook money, and time deposits) totaled $350 billion. In the last ten years (to 1977) the Federal Reserve System has allowed the money supply to increase by $512 billion in the United States and has exported some $600 to $800 billion overseas. This deflation of the dollar's value has led to the beginning of the drop of the value of the dollar on the world market. The dollar is being forsaken as the standard for world trade, which has contributed to the mass buying of gold and the shocking rise in its value. Fortunately many overseas dollars have been reinvested in U. S. Treasury securities and American holdings, but this will stop if the value of the dollar falls significantly.

Runaway inflation discourages productive work and money-saving and motivates further indebtedness. From 1970 to 1977 the productivity per man-hour in our country had a much slower growth than in the rest of the industrial world. The U. S. increase was 21%, Canada was 25%, Italy was 38%, Japan 47%, France 42%, and

Germany 46%. Inflation also decreases the motivation
to be honest. In Germany before Hitler, inflation resulted
in many women becoming prostitutes. For many, eating
becomes more important than morality.

The chief cause of inflation is greed, or idolatry. When
President Eisenhower was asked what he thought was
the cause and cure for inflation, he said, "That's easy.
The cause is the greed of the American people. The cure
is to curb the greed of Americans." Unless there is spiritual renewal, turning men away from idolatrous greed,
these trends will likely continue and accelerate.

William E. Simon, former Secretary of the Treasury,
chairman of the Economic Policy Board and of the Federal Energy Office, has brilliantly shown how close the
West, and especially America, is to economic trouble and
to loss of freedom in his book *A Time for Truth.*[2] The
objective facts he presents overwhelmingly show that the
selfish demands of all individual citizens have brought
us to a governmental crisis. He writes, "There is . . . a
substantial awareness in our political leadership that our
fiscal and economic policies have gone awry and that
the multiple promises of cradle-to-grave security for our
citizens can no longer be responsibly expanded, if indeed
they can be fulfilled. This is true not only in America,
but also in all the Western social democratic nations that
are guided by the same egalitarian-redistributionist philosophy. . . . I had countless private conferences with the
leaders of those nations. . . . Chiefs of state and finance
ministers of America's Western allies told me with great
concern that they no longer knew how to sustain the
levels of economic support which their citizens had come
to believe was their 'right.' All were counting on America
to save them. But America was in the same position."
He warns, "Unless the lethal pattern is changed—which
means, unless the philosophy that shapes this pattern is
changed—this nation will be destroyed." He points out

that, unrecognized by the public, there has been laid "the groundwork for an economic dictatorship which is expanding geometrically year after year." He says, "We are careening with frightening speed toward collectivism and away from individual sovereignty, toward coercive centralized planning and away from free individual choices, toward a statist-dictatorial system and away from a nation in which individual liberty is sacred."

Mr. Simon sees the answer in a return to the free enterprise capitalistic system. Corporations have responded to him by endowing about thirty academic centers and chairs of free enterprise. But can such a system work in conditions where individual selfishness and dishonesty prevail? The free enterprise system worked when the controlling philosophy was belief in God, when there was ethical honesty derived from this, and when concern for others was prominent. But we have shown that the growth of selfish individualism is what brings governmental chains to the free enterprise system. (cf. pp. 86, 87).

The exaltation of the individual who selfishly amassed great wealth produced the regulating bureaucracy. Total government employment has gone from six million persons in 1949 to sixteen million in 1979 and continues to increase.[3] They are there to satisfy the public and regulate abuse. This bureaucracy continues regardless of who is in political control and therefore they tend to do what they wish. They are a dominating branch of government that our founders never envisioned or intended. They are there primarily because of American greed and dishonesty. They are the chief hindrance to free enterprise.

If the people of America continue down the road of greed or idolatry, the destination can hardly be any other than more extreme individualism, an increase in the breakdown of relationships between men and women, a continual decline in morals, and a loss of productive labor. Unless this is stopped by spiritual renewal, the free enterprise system will not work, the bureaucracy will grow and we will proceed toward dictatorship.

Mammon Worship and Racial and International Tensions

The racial problem in the United States has centered primarily around the economic issue. Since 1954, when the legal barriers began to go down between whites and blacks, the main concern of blacks has been toward gaining economic opportunity, and this is still the foremost issue.

The black efforts have produced a much larger black middle class. For example, in 1954 the number of black families earning the equivalent of $25,000 or more in 1977 purchasing power was one in two hundred, while today it is one in eleven. There is a growing income gap in the black community, with many becoming richer and many others becoming poorer. Moreover, the overall gap between blacks and whites is getting larger again. There was an initial indication of an increase in the median income of blacks as compared to whites, but now the trend is reversing. The income of black families as a percentage of white-family income increased from 53% to almost 63% in 1975, but by 1977 the trend had reversed and the percentage declined to 57%. There is thus a widening gap in the median income between whites and blacks. The improvement from 1963 to 1975 came to a large extent because of legal governmental pressure to hire blacks and not entirely because of improvement of black ability to do productive work. This may have therefore been artificial and temporary. There is also a growing gap in employment. In 1954 only four percentage points separated jobless figures for whites and blacks, but in 1978 the gap was 22 percentage points.

I am convinced that the source of the economic problem

for the black community is the high rate of one-parent families—especially matriarchal families. Black families with both husband and wife declined from 77.7% in 1950 to 56.1% in 1978. The proportion of female-headed black families grew from 17.6% in 1950 to 39.2% in 1978. If the black male leadership would exalt sexual chastity and life-long marriage with male spiritual leadership, it would do more than anything else to transform black people into a productive and prosperous community. But if present trends of disparity between blacks and whites continue, when a big economic crisis comes it could lead to the worst racial conflict ever experienced in the United States.[4]

The Hispanic population is much stronger in its families in most areas of the U. S. Those of this origin increased 14.3% in the last five years and at present rates will become the largest minority group in the U. S. in ten years. It probably will become more influential economically than blacks because of its family stability.

The greed of Americans and other western nations may be the most significant matter in *foreign* as well as domestic issues. Jesse Jackson, one of our most influential black leaders, has said, "It's this gulf between wealth and poverty that threatens world peace."[5]

The United States has 6% of the world population, yet it consumed 32% of all energy in the world in 1973. According to Ronald Sider, "There are fifty-five times more goods and services available per person in the United States than in India. If one divides up the world into a rich one-third and a poor two-thirds, then the rich 34% claims 87% of the world's total GNP each year. The poor two-thirds is left with 13%.

"Virtually all authorities agree that the chasm will widen greatly by the year 2000. . . . Differences in income per head between the poor and the rich countries were around 1:2 at the beginning of the nineteenth century;

they are around 1:40 today in nominal or around 1:20 in real terms!"[6]

The nations above the thirtieth parallel (generally speaking) are white and rich. Those below are colored and poor. As the disparity in food and goods grows, a world-wide racial explosion becomes a real possibility. It is the poverty of third and fourth world countries that makes them so open to Communism. America will have to solve the problem of economic greed or find itself in military conflict to keep Communism from taking over the American continents. This will be a ready-made situation demanding a dictatorial militaristic leadership.

Disintegration of Male Creative Work and of Labor Relations

It has been shown that creative work which is distinguished as "man's work" is necessary for men to feel needed and to experience a vital social identity. Otherwise men will drop out of society and even become anti-social to gain recognition (in Chapter Three, pp. 36–38). The male will then focus more intently on the sex act for selfish individual pleasure and conquest.

Strangely enough, the brilliant scientific and technological society which American men have built is fast losing its creative and also its specific male nature. The work has become more impersonally organized, more computerized, and more mechanized because men in management positions have so designed it to increase their profits. Except for a proportionately few men, special skills or intellectual abilities or masculine muscle is not used on the job. Now men push a button, repeatedly perform the same boring tasks, or simply follow routine specifications. A man is a number lost in a big organization. Even in agriculture the great corporations are taking over the land and working it with larger and more mechanized and computerized equipment.

Men have done so much to make their jobs easier and more efficient that the full strength of a man is often no longer required. A woman can even load a pile of logs by pushing the right levers. Women have flooded into every job that was masculine and by court orders have pushed open almost every job gate marked "men." Women reporters can even go into the locker rooms to scoop the athletic stories. More and more women are entering the work force, and men are meeting them with resentment, seduction, and inequities, while the men are less satisfied and are dropping out. The change in the percentage of men and women in the work force is affected both by women entering and men leaving. In 1960 the work force was 67% men and 33% women while today it is 59% men and 41% women.

As a result of the growth of individual selfishness through distorted roles, the world of business and industry is facing a new crisis. The new workers are dissatisfied, highly individualistic, demanding of their rights, and rebellious against authority. The new breed of worker is dedicated to his or her own prosperity and comfort. They are "skeptical, often arrogant and demanding." There are "frequent clashes between [them and] the old-line management. . . . productivity is rising at a much slower pace. Absenteeism is a problem, and job turnover has reached a record level. Some workers have taken their complaints against the boss to court and to congress." Ted Mills, director of the American Center for the Quality of Work Life in Washington, D. C., says, "If we do not cope with this in the next decade, our industrial society is in serious trouble."[7]

A Michigan Survey Research Center study showed, "Sixty percent of the workers surveyed want new jobs.

Thirty-nine percent think they are underpaid. Thirty-six percent say they have unused skills, thirty-six percent feel overqualified for their jobs, and fifty-five percent want more time off."[8]

Rebellion toward authority is growing. An Opinion Research Corporation poll showed, "In 1969, 70% of the young accepted authority with few reservations. Now [1979], 70% say they need not take orders from a supervisor." The American Civil Liberties Union's biggest caseload now involves worker complaints against employers. Director Ira Glasser says, "There is an employee rights movement underway in this country."[9] Congress and state legislatures are receiving more complaints and requests for legislation to benefit the employee than ever before.

At the root of this is a strong individualism which does not necessarily work through organized labor unions. Rosabeth Kanter of Yale University suggests, "We are witnessing a predominantly individual phenomenon, a change in job holders' views of what they are entitled to rather than an increase in strident demands or organized activism."[10]

Unionized labor was 27% of the work force in 1957 and only about 21% in 1977. In National Labor Review Board elections labor won 65% in 1957 and only about 47% in 1977. "The Me generation has taken over the workplace, forcing big business, big labor, and big government all to look for new ways to fit its *individualistic* members into the economic system" (italics mine).[11]

With the man increasingly facing a loss of identity in the sex act by the breakdown of long-term sexual relations in marriage and a loss of identity through creative work, men are subsconsciously desperate for some role that distinguishes them. The rough team sports, especially football, have become a major point of male identity by participation either actively or vicariously from the stands or by television. Football exalts physical violence, organization, and secrecy of the huddle. Football is a good sport, but in high school and above, it has become more brutal each year. James Garrick of the University of Washington Sports-Medicine Dept., in a *New York Times* Syndicate Survey in 1975, pointed out that football injures a million and a half youngsters each autumn, and if there were a disease of such epidemic proportions, "Americans would revolt." James A. Michener has called football "the American form of violence."[12] Football could become for America what the brutal boxing and wrestling matches in the Palaestra at the Olympics were for the Greeks and what the gladiator shows were for Rome.

Is the scene being set in America for proliferation of male gangs or for some dynamic militaristic leader to call young men to the brutal task of war to prove their manhood? One can feel the overtones in America similar to those of the times prior to Philip of Macedon in Greece, of Julius Caesar in Rome or before Hitler in Germany.

Selfish Individualism Affects the Political Process

The distortion of roles is also the most evident reason for the growth of the selfish individualism that is fragmenting America and affecting the whole political process. Kevin Phillips has recently pointed out in his article, "The Balkanization of America," that loyalties of people are narrowing and society is dissolving. He shows that the fragmentation in society is causing fragmentation in government that now can no longer just be attributed to political rivalries. He says, "For the past several years the symptoms of decomposition have appeared throughout the body politic—in the economic, geographic, ethnic, religious, cultural, and biological sectors of society. Small loyalties are replacing larger ones. Small outlooks are also replacing larger ones."[13]

People are realizing more and more that self-interest

groups are becoming a threat to the nation. *U. S. News and World Report* has commented, "There is worry that the growing emphasis on group rights has shattered the once-vaunted American sense of common identity and purpose that gave credibility to the 'melting pot' as a national success story. Today that sense of oneness is cracking under the pressure of on-rushing claims of many kinds. . . ."[14] If a great economic crisis should strike, as it will if trends are unchanged, this fragmentation will become more intense and violent, especially by lower income people toward the more prosperous.

Selfish Individualism and Civil Injustice

Selfish individualism is so dominant in America that the rights of the individual criminal are repeatedly favored over those of society. In recent years the emphasis has been on protecting the individual criminal's rights—on making him or her comfortable, sanitary, and content, and on rehabilitation—rather than on protecting society. The courts and parole systems have sent back into the streets criminals who repeat their crimes. Because so many criminals are quickly released, this tends to undermine police work. Because of the high cost of police training and equipment and the increased costs of imprisonment (estimated to be $15,000 to $18,000 per year per prisoner), police forces are diminishing under strained budgets and the courts and parole boards are under pressure to free all but the most serious offenders as soon as possible. Crime cost the public ninety billion dollars in 1974, and is much more per year now.

Several studies have shown that, at least for the repeater, strict justice is the only way to reduce crime. Francis B. Looney, a deputy police commissioner of New York City; Chesterfield Smith, former president of the American Bar Association; Frank Carrington, executive director of Americans for Effective Law Enforcement, and others have come to this conclusion. Former Attorney General Saxbe has bluntly stated, "Rehabilitation is a 'myth.'"

The rights of the individual have been so exalted that public sentiment has been against capital punishment. The laws for capital punishment were not equitably applied, for various reasons, such as liberal sentiments for criminals by some judges and not by others and the lack of clarity of many of these laws. This resulted in the 1972 Supreme Court ruling that capital punishment constituted cruel and unjust punishment. However, many states have improved and clarified their laws on capital punishment, and it is again legal. But the sentiment for the individual is so much stronger than concern for social good that men are cruelly held for years awaiting death and there is talk of a federal law prohibiting capital punishment. Strangely enough, I have found that the very people who advocate abolition of capital punishment are often the ones who are strongly for abortion—the murder of innocent unborn infants who cannot defend themselves.

Some say the death sentence is wrong because it involves taking the life of one who is made in the image of God. The Bible teaches the opposite—if a man kills another man who is made in the image of God, that man should die (Genesis 9:6). God's glory and the protection of innocent society are the motives.

If a law is passed ruling out the death sentence for crime, the whole legal system could then become anti-Christian. *The heart of the Christian message is based on the justice of the death sentence.* The Bible teaches that the wages of sin is death and that God was so committed to the just punishment of those who transgressed His will that in order to forgive man He sent His Son to bear the death penalty for guilty men. If such a law is passed, selfish individualism could so dominate over religious and social good that innocent people, especially Christians, might be persecuted.

More and more large cities are facing economic difficulties, and with the growth in crime they are unable to cope with the problem. Former U. S. Attorney General Saxbe has warned that if we go on as we are, the nation may be driven to a national police force, which could be dangerous as a possible instrument of national repression.[15] The economic conditions of big cities such as New York, Cleveland, and Atlanta have caused reduction in police forces to dangerous levels, and in emergencies they have already frequently required state patrol or National Guard help. The direction we are moving in is clear—a national police force.

Individualism Destroys Meaningful Marriage Benefits

Public Acceptance of Sex for Selfish Individual Pleasure

Marriage for meaningful sexual relations is disappearing. Sex for selfish pleasure is now the accepted norm. *Secret immorality* began to be widely practiced in the early nineteenth century. By about 1900, under the impact of the thinking of Sigmund Freud, Havelock Ellis and others, and also of the motion picture industry and lowered literary standards, the United States entered the phase of an appeal for *open-mindedness*. In the 1960's the final breakdown of all barriers was attained and the phase of *everything should be legal* began. Sexual milestones were reached, such as openness of homosexuals (1968), allowing sex acts on the screen if the play has "redeeming social value" (as the U. S. Supreme Court ruled concerning *I Am Curious (Yellow)*), toplessness, bottomlessness, and even a California court ruling that heterosexual sex performed on a platform (stage) is acceptable as art. The full exposure of bodies in both homosexual and heterosexual acts is now permissible for "adult" viewers.

Selfish sex pleasure is a commodity to advertise and promote, and each motion picture studio, T.V. programmer, and advertiser is seeking to outdo the others in reaching the limit that the public conscience will allow. That conscience is gradually becoming weaker.[16]

In every major U. S. city there are clubs where hundreds of couples come to swap and go to bed with whomever they choose. Social parties including top leaders of business and civil government with men and women at times have entertainment displaying the body completely naked. The sex revolution in the United States is about complete.

In the United States the advocating of sex for selfish personal pleasure apart from responsible marriage emerged with strong philosophical arguments in the second quarter of the twentieth century. There have always been a number of people in the U. S. who have advocated this point of view, but not as a serious option to replace married sex as a norm. But in our time there has arisen the Playboy philosophy for men and the free girl philosophy for women.

About twenty-five years ago Hugh Hefner began to advocate the idea that men should make sex for pleasure a chief objective. This came to mean using women for their pleasure as sex objects. This Playboy philosophy leads to rejecting the responsibilities of marriage and children. A pregnant woman is incongruous with that thinking. The extremist fits children in only to use them for sex pleasure also. The philosophy of Hefner has been spread by Larry Flynt and many others. Its link to big business and politics has grown and reached tremendous proportions. Supply women to men as entertainment and they will do business with you or they will use their political influence for your benefit. All the details of how to be a playboy have been placed in neat handbooks of how to do it.[17]

Women who have accepted a selfish individualist view of life have adopted this same more masculine short-range view of sex. Helen Gurley Brown has given the single girl all the details of how to enjoy sex without marriage. She is said to "torpedo the myth that a girl must be married to have a satisfying life."[18] The assumption is that a girl can sleep around with various men and be very happy. The more "free" women there are available to men, the easier it becomes for immoral men to talk others into joining them. Long-range married sex is becoming a passe lifestyle.

The ultimate terminus of that view is—why have a man at all? Those of that view claim that masturbation or lesbianism may allow greater freedom and pleasure. According to Shere Hite, orgasm by masturbation may be just as acceptable as intercourse as a way to go for women. Unfortunately her survey centered on the mailing list of the National Organization for Women that has the feminist bias. She concluded there is only *one form of orgasm* and that there is no difference between orgasm without intercourse and that with it.[19]

On the other hand, Dr. Marie Robinson and other skilled psychiatrists have found that the fullest and deepest orgasm by women is achieved only when they completely surrender to a man in intercourse. They have been repeatedly successful at leading women who could not enjoy that full experience to solve their hostilities toward men so that they release themselves and experience a more complete satisfaction. Dr. Robinson, Dr. Marynia Farnham, and others have shown that it is precisely those women who want to go it alone and who have hostilities toward men who cannot achieve this.[20]

Since Shere Hite's study was subsidized by the National Organization for Women (N.O.W.) and her survey was made by women sympathetic to those views, it was biased. Even though those taking her survey would be more inclined toward a selfish view of sex, much of the testimony she gives about orgasm shows that women desire something deeper than clitoral stimulation. She seems to present her study as the first authentic study of women and the best authority for women. She concludes that for women to find sexual happiness they should seek to free themselves from dependence on men.

The inevitable conclusion of Ms. Hite's views must be that self-masturbation, which requires no surrender by the woman, is the best way—that is the only way for complete independence. While Ms. Hite implies this she avoids clearly stating it. Because her view is erroneous, women will continue to want men. But if they accept the view that sex is for selfish pleasure, women will accept sexual immorality, masturbation, and other male short-term ideas of sex. The women's movement, like the Playboy philosophy for men, has led us to a perilous point of selfish individualism in this view of sex.

Resultant Male Attitudes Toward the Family

The recent "Playboy Report on American Men" by Louis Harris (and other studies by Dr. Joshua S. Golden, director of the human sexuality program at U. C. L. A.) shows that American men are *ideally* conservative toward maintaining the traditional family, with 84% of those surveyed saying they think the family is very important. But many of these have actually abandoned those things which make meaningful family life possible. They want the benefits of the family without the responsibilities which make it worthwhile and stable. Marriage and the family have rather become tools for selfish fulfillment. According to the poll, many men no longer desire to spend their free time with their spouses, share friends, or practice religion at home. Only two out of five wanted children and 58% of these considered two or less children ideal. Only one out of four desired a stable sex life, and less than half considered sex "very important." A majority were not willing to sustain a bad marriage and seek to improve it for the children's sake.

There are several implications which may be deduced from this survey. Male selfishness, which is the chief cause of the feminist movement, is evident. Also, negative attitudes in men toward female companionship, sex, and the responsibility of children seem to have resulted from competitive attitudes of modern women.

Sexual promiscuity by men became evident in the early nineteenth century but has become widespread in our time. In recent years the scandal of sexual irresponsibility in high places dramatizes and promotes the failure of men to be faithful. In the political arena we have had the disclosures of John F. Kennedy's affairs, Joan Kennedy's frank talk about those of her husband Ted, and news stories about leading legislators such as Wilbur Mills and Wayne Hays. These and many others are unveiled in the book *Fishbait,* by "Fishbait" Miller. Divorce and remarriage by prominent politicians, until recently a political liability, is now common.

Women's "Lib" or Vulnerability?

Loss of Protection. Conditions are developing that will put women in positions where they will suffer severely. Male structures for protecting women in the home, at school, and at work are being torn down. Government legal protections for women, such as child custody, alimony and inheritance rights, are being changed. In March, 1979, in Alabama and in April, 1979, in New York, the courts made alimony payable by women as well as men. These rulings have made the male supremacy laws suspect in the states. Louisiana repealed a 200-year-old statute on this in 1978, and now other states have similar bills pending. More and more courts are awarding child custody to men, whereas until recently children were almost always awarded to the mother.

As women compete in the home, men become frustrated and respond in ways that make women even more abused and unhappy. When they lose respect and identity as the family leader, men seek to compensate by sexual conquest and violent use of their superior physical force. New Hampshire University studies indicate six million wives are regularly beaten annually. Another study estimates there is some beating of 28 million.[21]

Men are also taking advantage of women's unprotected position by seducing women working with them or pressuring women to have sex in order to secure their jobs or gain advancement. For example, Al Ripskis, publisher of "Impact," a newsletter, and an employee of H. U. D., made an unofficial survey within the Department of Housing and Urban Development. About thirty-eight percent of those responding said they had been coerced or enticed by their boss to have sex in order to obtain job advancement. Three out of ten said they gave in. Fifty percent of those refusing said they suffered in job assignments as a consequence.[22] And men are taking advantage of unprotected women by enslaving an increasing number in prostitution.[23]

Loss of Marriage Love. Women are expressing their hostilities in the turmoil of competition in the home. Roger Longley and Richard Levy in a new study estimate that 12 million wives assault their husbands annually, which is about 20% of the total married women.[24] As love and affection disintegrate in the home, women are denying their husbands conjugal rights. As a result, New Jersey, Delaware, Iowa, and Oregon have adopted laws that allow spouses to file rape charges against their mates.

As a woman fights for equality in terms of selfish independence, she creates greater hostilities that destroy marriage happiness, and as she gains more independence she becomes more and more the victim of unprincipled men and loses her protection from their abuses.

Loss of Desire for Children. In the midst of such hostility and insecurity, women more and more reject the normal feminine desire to have children. This forces up the number of childless women, abortions, and all kinds of child abuse. The feelings of guilt and the realization that motherhood has been misused or poorly handled have created tremendous psychological problems. Moreover, investigations show that in about one out of three instances of abortion, women are using doctors and clinics that are incompetent, abusive, or money-making outfits.[25] This can hardly be called liberation for women.

An anti-child attitude is increasingly evident among women. Betty Rolin, N. B. C. newscaster, has said, "Motherhood is in trouble, and it ought to be. The rude question is long overdue: who needs it?" Her attitude is that of a growing army of women in America. The fertility rate per woman has been decreasing consistently, showing a diminishing desire for children. The number of children per woman was 8 in early America, 6 by 1850, 4 by 1900, 3.7 in 1960, 2.5 in 1970, and 1.9 in 1975. The present rate produces less than zero population growth. Women who ran away from their children was one or two percent in 1976 but had reached about five percent in 1978.

Studies by the World Bank, the World Health Organization, and Brookings Institute all show that breast-feeding is important for better health of a child, and doctors now widely recommend this. But from 1963 to 1973 the number of American mothers suckling babies when they left the hospital had dropped 50 percent.

An increasing number of women are concerned more

about working to earn money than about caring for their children or husbands. About thirty percent of all wives with preschool children worked with outside jobs in 1975, and a majority of women with school children did. It is estimated that 57 out of 100 women will be working outside the home by 1990.[26] Having a higher living standard is given greater priority than forming human relationships and developing well-adjusted people. According to a study by the University of Michigan Survey Research Center in 1957, one-fourth of employed wives said they would prefer to be at home, but only three percent gave that answer recently (1979), and these were primarily those with preschool children. However, in spite of feeling guilty, housewives indicated they enjoyed their work. Women composed 33 percent of the work force in 1960 and 41 percent in 1979.

Those trying to promote women's rights have taken unreasonable steps to get women into jobs by governmental force. For example, in 1979 the La Grange, Georgia, police force was told it would be denied federal funds unless it gave 46 percent of its jobs to women, that being the percentage of women in the labor force of the community.

Not Freedom, but Double Jobs Requiring Superwoman. The vision of freedom for women as advocated by the feminists is not working out as they planned. Women envisioned being freed from their "menial" work in the home, or at least of sharing it with their husbands so they could spend most of their time in making a lot of money in the market place. But every study done thus far shows that women have instead ended up with two jobs—with the home responsibilities as well as their public job earning money.

This has happened because the male ego does not respond to assuming "women's work" and also because women don't want to give up the job in the home because of the influence or power it gives them with their children and husbands. Moreover, their wage-earning jobs have produced only 60% of what men earn for their public employment. Apparently the public mind still naturally accepts the idea that the man's job should receive recognition as being of greater importance (cf. pp. 32, 33, 36–38).

Hence women are having to be "superwomen" to fulfill their double role of housewife and wage earner, and for little financial gain. In a speech by Betty Friedan in New York in November, 1979, she decried these conditions which have resulted and said, "We told our daughters, 'you can have it all.' Well, can they have it all? Only by being superwoman. Well, I say no to superwoman!" So instead of freedom, women have in general ended up with greater servitude.

Becoming a Matriarch or God. Some women in America not only want to have equal authority with men, but their hate has led them to proclaim openly that they want to rule over men. Feminist leaders Costanza, Steinem, Millett and others were the speakers for a forum in New York City on October 1, 1978, attended by about 1400 militant women advocating matriarchy. Their main speaker was Senator Edward Kennedy. They expressed the desire not only to gain equality but to put women in the place of power in the home, in the churches, and in other institutions. Their slogan was, "We who nurture will govern." Tee shirts with the message, "Matriarchy is the Answer," were sold. The meeting was filled with shouting, foot stomping, and high emotion. They ended with a song entitled "A Feminist Prayer." It started, "Our Mother, which art in heaven," and ended, "A-women."[27] The Lord's prayer is now being led publicly in this manner in churches all across America by humanistic clergymen.

Already many women pursuing the role of equality (in terms of sameness) are advocating the return to the worship of degrading female deities of the ancient world.

In April, 1978, four hundred feminists met for a three-day seminar course on "The Great Goddess Reemerging," at the University of California campus in Santa Cruz. Christine Winter, head of the religious studies department at San Diego University, believes these feminists are "willing to replace the biblical God with a frankly pagan and polytheistic approach." When one studies the degraded sex orgies and temple prostitution involved in these religions, it seems clear that some feminist leaders are moving down the same road that reduced women to their most tragic conditions of the past.

In going back to ancient goddesses these women are seeking to exalt the female image in such a way as to promote the worship of material wealth and pleasure instead of God. In so doing they are following the leadership of the men who initiated the decline of society by pursuing these goals. In so doing they are denying their distinctive feminine creative power in favor of creating *exclusively* like men.

Motherhood Without Women and Women Without the Feminine? The ultimate end of the women's liberation movement can be more drastic than any of us would dare dream. As George Gilder said, "We are very close to a small step for man—a giant leap for mankind—over a genetic precipice."[28]

The new genetic technology which has primarily emerged within the last thirty years has added eight new possible options as to how humans are born. They are (1) artificial insemination of a wife by her husband; (2) artificial insemination of a woman by a donor; (3) ovarian, or egg, transplant from one woman to another and subsequent artificial insemination by either the husband or a select donor; (4) fertilization of an egg in vitro (in glass) followed by implantation into a woman; (5) extracorporeal gestation (or conceiving and raising a baby in a test tube); (6) parthenogenesis (virgin birth or the development of an unfertilized egg); (7) nuclear transplant, or cloning, in which a cell is made to produce an exact genetic duplicate of the donor of the nucleus, male or female; (8) embryo fusion, or the joining together of two individual embryos to form a human with four biological parents instead of the traditional two.[29] Dr. Joseph Lederbert has said essentially all these can be accomplished in the next ten to thirty years. About half of these are now possible in whole or in part on some basis.

All of these forms of reproduction completely remove the need for any direct relationship between the man and the woman. In some of them the mother still may carry and bear the baby, giving her a continuing relationship, but she *may* delegate that responsibility to another woman who is not the mother. If extracorporeal gestation, or test-tube babies, is developed, the woman need have *no relationship to the child* other than furnishing the egg. Such genetic engineering may completely remove any need for sexual relations of men and women for procreation, and the woman could leave bearing and raising children to the state for its complete control. The man, and possibly even the woman, could be denied any identity with the child.

Dr. Daniele Petrucci, an Italian biologist, fertilized a human egg and allowed it to grow outside the human body for fifty-nine days, even attaining a heartbeat, but had to destroy it because it became deformed. Russian scientists who learned from Petrucci have kept many embryos alive for six months. Already babies born 3 months early have been kept alive by artificial means, so that completion of a birth outside the mother is close.

The official Chinese newspaper *Jenmin Jin Pao* of the Peoples Republic of China applauded Petrucci and said, "If children can be had without being born, working mothers need not be affected by childbirth. This is happy news for women." Such a breakthrough would obviously become a prime objective of the women's movement and would be backed up by government under the ERA. But the women would become the prime losers. The essence of femininity, namely the woman's creation of the child within, would be done away. Only the male concept of short-term pleasurable sex would prevail under state control, and that could be by masturbation or homosexuality. Thus the need for marriage or family or even any contact with the opposite sex could be eliminated.

The feminine is that which represents the loving, tender caring in humans, and it is the submission of the man to the female sexual control that modifies his aggressiveness and helps him to have social concern and love. Under genetic engineering or control of births that removes women's influence in childcare and marriage the state could then become in charge of a society that would likely be mercilessly militaristic and masculine. "When you want to create a solidaristic group of male killers, that is what you do, you kill the woman in them. That is the lesson of the Marines."[30]

Since there are indications the United States is moving economically and every other way toward a statist dictatorship, this poses a fearful possibility. The possibility of genetic engineering of a master race such as Hitler dreamed of and sought, is now fast emerging (cf. Howard and Rifkin, *Who Should Play God?*), and it will almost certainly be male-directed and controlled.

It will be male-dominated since over 90 percent of our scientists and most of our politicians are men. Women could become the pawns for sex pleasure and instruments of labor in a man's world, having no unique feminine worth. The natural desires of women to have a family and raise children could be completely erased by men or masculinized women.

"Here begins to emerge the real menace of women's liberation. By reducing the realm of sexual constitution, one does not create a new realm of groovy communal love. One creates a vacuum in the lives of the people. Individuals no longer so closely tied to mother, family, and sexuality become more open to a totalitarian state— a state with powers, moreover, unapproached by any government in all human history."[31]

But could such a situation ever emerge in the United States? Our minds are being prepared and we are placing the government in position to have that kind of control. Howard and Rifkin have shown how fast and far the United States has moved toward eugenic controls and how many prominent scientists have advocated these methods as the quickest way to improve our nation and move toward supermen.[32]

Eugenics as a way of controlling crime became popular in the U. S., with at least 16 states passing laws giving police power to sterilization of unwanted types. These laws were upheld by the Supreme Court. The theory behind these fell into disrepute at the end of the first quarter of the twentieth century. However, with the discovery of the structure of DNA new proposals have been made to control crime.[33] Some lawmakers are proposing that welfare problems be solved by eugenics.

In almost every state voluntary birth control by sterilization has become legal and popular. Along with this, modern birth control pills that affect body hormones and prohibit ovulation, and the use of the IUD, which is a form of abortion, have been widely accepted. Also the Supreme Court has legalized abortion. Thus, whether good or bad, medical procedures affecting the conception and birth of children are now prevalent and popular. Through them mental resistance to scientific and governmental interference has been reduced.

Moreover, artificial insemination of animals for improving them is accepted practice. Presently 95% of all cattle (over sixty million) and many other animals (fifty million ewes, one million sows, 125,000 mares, 60,000 goats, and four million turkeys) regularly are born this way in the U. S.[34] Embryo transplants are now common among animals. Frozen sperm and even embryo banks for animals are common. Choice animals are selected and improved this way. Hence, the validity of biological improvement by genetic engineering is accepted in the public mind. Our school systems teach that man is only the highest animal in the evolutionary process, and if men and women begin to act like uncontrolled animals it would be an easy step to apply these things to man.

A serious national, economic and criminal crisis in America would make it easy for the government to lead the people down the road of accepting these practices in humans as a solution. Hitler's program seemed harmless at first, but became a nightmare the German people could not remove. Are we so naive as to think this can't happen to us?

The ultimate step of control, as advocated by some behavioristic psychology, which has been taught in our colleges for years, would then become reality. As animals, human life would be under the control of a few powerful men, as advocated by B. F. Skinner, Harvard psychologist.[35]

Although few Americans are aware of it, many of our greatest scientists are advocating such extremes. Nobel laureate Sir Francis Crick, discoverer of DNA and one of the chief genetic engineers, has said, ". . . No newborn infant should be declared human until it has passed certain tests regarding its genetic endowment and . . . if it fails these tests it forfeits the right to live." Nobel laureate Linus Pauling has suggested there should be tattooed on the forehead of every young person a symbol showing his genotype so the marriage of those with defective genes could be avoided.[36]

Then the rebellion of man's sinful nature would be complete. He will have not only taken over man's identity through creative work and woman's identity through having children, but he will have begun to play the role of God, saying who should live and who should die.

The Breakdown of the Family

Because relationships between men and women are so distorted, the family as the socializing unit is rapidly breaking down. Many statistics have been compiled by various groups showing the breakdown of the home. Some of the following were compiled by U. S. Representative Barbara A. Mikulski with Esther Laderer and published in *Ann Landers' Encyclopedia.* Others have been taken from U. S. census reports, from news magazines such as *U. S. News and World Report,* and a few other sources.[37] I have reorganized them for presentation in the rest of this chapter. While I have not been able to check them all, I believe they are reasonably accurate.

Tensions within the family are growing. One out of every four murders in the United States occurs within the family, and one of every two of these is between the husband and wife. One out of four couples engage in violence. A poll showed that 20% of the American people approve of one spouse hitting the other, and that figure rises to 25 percent of those with college education or above.

Sex without marriage is increasingly preferred. In 1970 there were 650,000 people living together out of wedlock who were willing to register this with the census. By 1977 this had risen to 1.5 million. Many more were doing so but without public acknowledgment. *Newsweek* has estimated there are probably six million people living together out of wedlock, which would be a six-fold increase since 1970.[38] There is an eight-fold increase for those under 25 years of age. According to studies by Johns Hopkins School of Hygiene and Public Health, in 1971 55% of American girls had sexual intercourse by age 19, and by 1976 the percentage was 63.3. For black girls the percentage was 82.8, but the biggest increase—ten percent—was among white girls.

Divorce has become easier to get. Before the Civil War divorce was exceedingly rare in the U. S. and often required legislative action. In 1870 there was only one divorce for every 33.7 marriages. During the marching years of the early wave of feminism (1900–1933), divorce began to be prevalent. It declined some for about ten years after World War II (1946–1956). It grew again after about 1957. The quick divorce in Nevada and other places undermined the standards of most states. The attitude became, "Why fight divorce when people can go elsewhere and get them?" There were 413,000 divorces in 1962 and 851,000 in 1973. In 1960 one of every four marriages ended in divorce; in 1978, one out of two (1.1 million divorces and 2.2 million marriages). Two out of three are predicted for 1990 at the present rates of change.[39] On January 1, 1970, California passed the first no-fault divorce law, and this has spread to 48 other states. The divorce rate rose 44 percent from 1970 to 1978. Recently New York began allowing the obtaining of divorces in department stores, and in March, 1979, California passed a law allowing do-it-yourself divorce by mail, thereby bypassing all courts, if there are no children. This will soon become the law throughout the United States—some twelve states began considering it in the first month after its passage. No doubt this will be extended in a short time to cases where children are involved, if past trends are followed, and the rate of divorce could accelerate even more.

The Tragic Effects on Children

The children are the main victims of role distortion and selfish individualism, and this can have lifelong effect. Those who are neglected and hurt because of a lack of love and meaningful relationships often become more selfish and violent than their parents. Thus "the iniquities of the fathers are visited upon the children to the third and fourth generations" (Exodus 20:5). This makes the future look very bleak indeed.

Neglect and Avoidance

Urie Bronfenbrenner and his associates refer to some thirty studies covering twenty-five years, most of which were made since World War II, that show American parents spend much less time with their children and are more permissive than in other nations. He says, "The generalization applies in such diverse areas as oral behavior, toilet accidents, dependency, sex aggressiveness, and freedom of movement outside the house." He shows that the American way of adults forsaking their children to the youth peer groups is a major cause for growth in antisocial behavior. Moreover, he points out that studies by Condry and Simon indicate that the age at which the peer group gains dominance over adult desired behavior has gotten lower in recent years.[40] Youth in America now spend two or three times as much time with their peers as with their parents.

He says, "We cannot escape the conclusion that, if the current trend persists, if the institutions of our society continue to remove parents and other adults and older youth from active participation in the lives of children, and if the resulting vacuum is filled by the age-segregated peer group, *we can anticipate increased alienation, indifference, antagonism, and violence on the part of the*

*younger generation in all segments of our society—middle
class children as well as the disadvantaged . . .* If adults
do not once again become involved in the lives of children,
there is trouble ahead for American society."[41]

Step-Parents or One Parent

According to 1975 figures, more than thirty percent
of school-age children in the United States are living with
parents who have been divorced at least once. Because
of rising rates of divorce, desertion and illegitimacy, one-
sixth of all children under 18 years of age live in one-
parent families. Only 56 percent of black children are
living in households with two parents present, compared
with 88 percent of white children. One-parent families
are growing about twenty times faster than two-parent
families. Government aid to families with dependent
children went from $2.8 billion in 1968 to $10.7 billion
in 1978.

Yet psychiatrist Armand M. Nicholi II of Harvard
has said, "If any one factor influences the character development and emotional stability of an individual, it is the
quality of the relationship he or she experiences as a child
with *both* parents. Conversely, if people suffering from
severe nonorganic emotional illness have one experience
in common, it is the absence of a parent through death,
divorce, a time-demanding job, or for other reasons."[42]

Children Battered, Rejected, Suicidal, Pregnant, and Aborted

There were at least two million child-abuse cases in
1978. More children die of child-abuse than any disease.
There are now over 500,000 foster children, four times
the number in 1961. If one includes children in correc-
tional institutions and other institutions, the number of

children living without parents reaches 750,000. Only 3.1 percent of the half million have no living parents and two percent are retarded or handicapped. Fifty percent are there because of emotional or drinking problems of the parents, and an astonishing 31 percent are there because the parents do not want them.

More than one million children ran away in 1978 to escape physical abuse or sexual exploitation by their parents. Many of these have ended up as victims of pimps and prostitution rings. Death by violence for young adults (15–24 years old) accounted for nineteen percent of the increase in the death rate between 1960 and 1974. For those 15 to 24 years of age the suicide rate has doubled since 1965. Infanticide has increased at an alarming rate. Child pornography is growing rapidly. In Los Angeles alone more than 30,000 children, many under the age of five years, have been currently rented or sold by their parents for this purpose.

The Supreme Court made abortion legal in 1973 and in 1978 over 1.2 million babies were aborted. That was one abortion for every 2.8 live births. In Washington, D. C., there are more illegitimate births than legitimate ones, and more abortions than live births. In spite of (or partially because of) effective birth control methods and sex education in the public schools, pregnancies of 15 to 19-year-olds increased one-third from 1971 to 1976, reaching 600,000 per year. A 1979 study by the Stanford Research Institute showed that teen-age pregnancies cost the American taxpayer $8.3 billion a year. A majority of the pregnancies of black girls are illegitimate. The number of first pregnancies that were aborted doubled from 1971 to 1976. The number of illegitimate births in the U. S. has doubled since 1960, causing a swelling of welfare rolls. Yet H. E. W. has been known to sponsor sex education in public schools that does not even mention marriage.

In spite of our education, wealth, and medical knowledge, the United States has the fourteenth highest infant mortality rate in the world. Ten million of our children have no source of basic medical care.

Disregard or hate for children is growing. In 1978 Ann Landers polled her readers, and of 50,000 parents who replied, seventy percent said that if they could make the choice over again they would not have children. T. V. personality Hugh Downs, feminist Ellen Peck, and critic John Simon have formed the National Organization for Non-Parents, which openly promotes having no children. Since 1970 the population under 14 years old has shrunk by 6.4 million. Children are becoming a threatened and valuable species.

Freedom from Parents

Because of the many abuses against children by parents, there are many do-gooders who are taking the side of children and are trying to free children from parental control. This will weaken parental control in good families and do more harm than good in most cases. According to a 1979 letter published by Orin G. Hatch, U. S. senator from Utah, there is proposed legislation allowing a child to sue his parents for forcing him to go to church, one requiring parents to pay minimum wages to children for doing household chores, and another which would allow children to choose their parents. A "Child's Bill of Rights" written by Richard Farson and published in *Ms* magazine advocates that in many cases children be given rights to choose that are equal with adults and sometimes places their rights above those of adults and even above civil laws. Radicals sought to make use of 1979, as the International Year of the Child, to try to pass such laws. The Pro-Family Forum claims that the I. Y. C. was initiated in the United Nations by Communists.[43]

Child Worship

On the other hand many parents swing the pendulum too far to the other extreme of selfish unwholesome overvaluation of their children. The parent may be seeking to achieve identity for himself or herself through the child, or there may be guilt over failures, fear of failure, and fears over the above-mentioned conditions of abuse. Whatever the cause, extreme overvaluation of the child is growing. Robert Coles, child psychiatrist and author of *Children of Crisis* (3 volumes), has said, "They (children) are the only thing the parents believe in. They don't believe in God, or any kind of transcendence, and so they believe in their children. They are concerned with them almost in a religious way—which I think is unfortunate—as an extension of themselves. This is quite a burden for a child to experience. In that sense, it is not cruelty to children. It is paganism." [44] This overvaluation of children also is producing children who feel the lack of real love and are insecure and very selfish.

Parent Rejection

The number of children who hate is growing. Maryland researchers Dennis J. Madden and Henry T. Harbin, in a paper to the 1979 meeting of the American Psychiatric Association, said that one out of ten children between the ages of three and eighteen performed some sort of intentional violent act against their parents. One of the surprising things about the student unrest of the 1960's was that many of the protesting children who wanted to destroy the establishment were not from the poor and low-level income families; a good number were from the wealthy and upper middle classes. These were driven by the most vicious kind of hate, because they had not experienced real love in their homes.

Most of the cults of America are attracting hurting children who are looking for some meaningful family relationships. The cult offers a false sense of family atmosphere. This is true of the Children of God, Sun Myung Moon's Unification Church, the Way, and many others.

Child Exclusion

Hostility toward children is seen in many other ways. In recent years there has been a significant increase in the number of apartment complexes and even whole communities that restrict children. This of course puts further pressure on couples not to have children and creates a further anti-child mentality. A growing number of children are unattended because both parents are working, thereby increasing violence and resulting in more landlords who want to exclude children.

Crisis in Child Education

Increases in school budgets in America have been defeated in community after community. Wages of teachers who are highly educated professionals are lower than those for many jobs requiring much lower qualifications. The already declining schools are therefore threatened further. This unwillingness to support the schools reflects the attitude toward children.

The effects of the breakdown of the home are being extensively felt in the school systems. There has been a consistent yearly drop in college entrance test scores since 1963, according to the College Entrance Examination Board. The steady decline was observed not only in the Scholastic Aptitude Test (SAT) but also in tests administered by the American College Testing Program (ACT). Parents are inclined to blame the public school systems for this. No doubt the loss of any consistent organizing philosophy to interpret data due to the exclusion of the concept of God from the public schools and the removal of discipline of school children have been partly responsible.[45] A $750,000 study by the College Entrance Examining Board revealed several causes of the decline in aptitude test scores, but two main ones were the lack of discipline in the school and absenteeism.

The primary cause for the undisciplined nature of the child is the conflict in the home and the loss of love and male authority. Absenteeism is related to the problem of discipline. In the urban schools of our country, fifty percent of the children often may be absent from classes. The misconduct in class and absenteeism are discouraging to teachers and make it hard to keep capable people in the teaching profession.[46]

But worse, more than 60,000 teachers were known to have been assaulted in the schools in 1978, and if unreported instances were known it is thought the figure would be twice that. This involves beatings, knife cuttings, shootings, being pushed down the stairs, rapes and other violent crimes. Threats and intimidations also are frequent. This causes our school systems to lose more quality teachers and pushes our education system into deeper trouble. If we have less teachers of lower quality the problems with children will grow proportionately.

Child Neglect and Crime

The crime rate has grown greatly over the last twenty-five years. Since 1960, juvenile arrests for violent crime increased 283 percent. In 1964 there were 4.5 million crimes committed, and in 1974 there were 10 million. There has been an increase in violent crime again in 1979 and if competition between husbands and wives in the homes continues, this will worsen.[47] (cf. pp. 48, 49).

The increase of unwanted and undisciplined children

because of role distortion caused by greed has led to large and growing teen-age gangs, especially in the big cities. In the 1,000 cities of over 25,000 population more than half of the violent street crimes are committed by gangs of youth. Walter B. Miller of Harvard Law School's Center for Criminal Justice headed a recent study of the problem and says, "From evidence that's available, youth groups and youth gangs are accounting for a higher and higher percentage of serious crimes."[48] These gangs are becoming increasingly aggressive, and in the years ahead they may likely be found pillaging and assaulting in rich and prosperous neighborhoods as well as downtown areas. The growing danger of gangs has been brought to the public mind by the current motion picture *The Warriors*, a story of a united gang plan to take over New York City.

Escape and Search for Identity by Drugs

One of the consequences of the unhappiness of young people in America is the rising drug use. Drugs are an avenue of escape and an attempt to seek meaning in life. Drug usage by young people before World War II was almost insignificant. Since that time it has grown rapidly. Figures show the continued increase in marijuana use even in the last three years. The number of those from twelve to twenty-five who have used pot went from 20,340,000 in 1974 to 25,050,000 in 1977.

It appears that about twelve and a half million young people under the age of 25 were current users of pot in 1977, and its usage was rapidly rising. President Carter said that over 45 million Americans had tried pot by 1977. The percentage of use of marijuana in the thirty days prior to an inquiry for high school senior classes was 27.1 in 1975, and 35.4 in 1977. For alcohol it was 68.2 in 1975 and 71.2 in 1977.[49]

Greed for money has been a major reason for the growth of the drug traffic. According to Dr. Peter Bourn, the drug business is surpassed today by only two corporations. It is having tragic criminal and social effects. More homicides occur because of drugs than any other cause, other than domestic fights.

The growth of the use of drugs seems to go along with the breakdown of the family. Children who have no close relationship to their parents and are unloved lose their sense of identity. Hence, drugs and alcohol are an escape. The renowned psychiatrist William Glasser has shown that sexual promiscuity has been motivated not only by the biological drive but also by the desire to find a relationship to another human being that will give the person identity.[50] Glasser's counseling and experimentation have shown that when a youth fails to relate in a meaningful way sexually, he turns to drugs and alcohol as an escape.[51] Failure to know how to relate to the opposite sex may be a major cause of indulgence in drugs and alcohol. The growth of sexual promiscuity among women may be one of the main reasons for their increased use of drugs and alcohol.[52]

Normalization of Homosexuality—The End of the Sexes and of Society

Conflict of Parents, a Main Cause of Homosexuality

We have pointed out that homosexuality is basically antisocial. The causes of homosexuality have been much debated, and this is a problem of considerable complexity. However, I am convinced most homosexuality is a result of a rejection of gender caused by the person's fear or hate which results from hostilities usually (but not always) between the parents. Then when the person becomes involved in sexual experimentation in preadolescence or adolescence, he or she experiences the greatest emotional freedom for sexual pleasure with one of the same sex. If the person is involved long enough, this preference becomes habitual.

For example, a mother may selfishly dominate and shower affection on her son, competing for his love and criticizing her husband. The child may see himself as a competitor with the father and fear him. Or the mother may criticize masculine traits in her son because of her hostility toward men. The child therefore turns against his gender and feels nature has been unfair to him. There are many possible different combinations of fear and hate that can cause this gender rejection, with boys or girls.

Since sexual experimentation at preadolescent and adolescent ages is often with those of the same sex because of peer organization, the homosexual fixation can easily occur.

John Leo, in his essay on homosexuality in *Time,* refers to the repeated appearance of parental conflict in studies of homosexuals. He said, *"This finding has been consistent among researchers* who find homosexuals sick and those who find them well" (italics mine).[53] Daniel Cappon has said, "It is the lack of lovemaking between parents which does the damage.[54]

The result is that there is no acceptance or closeness of the child with the parent of the same gender. Peter and Barbara Wyden, in *Growing Up Straight,* researched all the homosexual studies up to that time (the year of the Stonewall revolt) and concluded that homosexuality *never* occurred in males when there was a close relationship between father and son.[55] Love between parents and for the children of the same gender could put an end to most homosexuality.

Moreover, many homosexuals can be redeemed. If the source of the fear and hate is resolved, the homosexual can then comfortably adopt a normal heterosexual lifestyle. Many have done this. But the homosexual must admit his or her need, be willing to turn from homosexual conduct, and seek support and help from others who care but have no lustful desires toward them. The emotional preference is habitual and hard to relinquish.

If the competition and conflict between the sexes continue to grow because of role distortions, homosexuality will surely continue to increase and become more openly insistent on its normalcy.

Normalization of Homosexuality?

Homosexuality has grown rapidly. Homosexuals have become publicly outspoken since the Stonewall revolt in June, 1968. They reacted to police tactics at Stonewall Tavern and held a mass public demonstration which led to a mass public disclosure by homosexuals. Since becoming a lobby group at that time, the homosexuals have persuaded the American Psychiatric Association to remove homosexuality from being considered abnormal conduct, which was done by a very narrow vote.

In referring to this, *Time* essayist John Leo has said, "In a highly political compromise, the A. P. A. adopted a statement declaring that 'homosexuality, per se, cannot be classified as a mental disorder.' The operative term, per se, left homosexuals free to think that they have been declared 'normal' and traditional psychiatrists free to think that homosexuality, though not a disorder itself, was, or could be, a symptom of underlying problems. To compound the confusion, the association felt that it had to list homosexuality somewhere, so it created a new diagnostic category, 'Sexual Orientation Disturbance,' for homosexuals dissatisfied with their sexuality . . . Though the A. P. A. vote seems to have pushed a great many therapists toward a more benign view of homosexuality, a strong body of psychiatric opinion still insistently holds that homosexuality reflects psychic disturbance. Last year an informed poll of 2,500 psychiatrists showed that a majority believed that homosexuals are sick."[56]

It has been pointed out that Betty Friedan and other women's leaders have been willing to include the homosexuals in the efforts for sexual equality (cf. p. 68). The gays have fought and won court cases to become recognized legitimate organizations on university campuses. They have organized their own homosexual religious denomination, the Universal Fellowship of Metropolitan Community Churches, with congregations in many cities, and are seeking acceptance as homosexuals in traditional church groups. These gay groups are Dignity (Roman Catholic), Integrity (Episcopal), Affirmation (United Methodist), The Catholic Coalition for Gay Civil Rights, Gay Mormons United, and Lutherans Concerned. The gay activists have plans to teach in the public schools that homosexual conduct is normal, if the Equal Rights Amendment is passed.

Already homosexuals *claim* they constitute one out of six persons in San Francisco, one out of fifteen in Atlanta, and so in other cities. Twenty-five thousand gays demonstrated in Washington, D. C., October 14, 1979. They have won court cases which prevent the armed forces from dismissing a person from service just because he is homosexual. Cities have elected homosexuals as known homosexuals to public office. Homosexual conduct is displayed in movies and on television as acceptable conduct. Masters and Johnson have portrayed them as the maximum lovers. A homosexual rights bill has been introduced in Congress by Rep. Ted Weiss (D-N. Y.). The trend is strongly toward normalization. If the trend does not change in a short time America may become like decadent Sodom and Gomorrah.

Endorsement of Incest?

One of the main abuses of children and a chief cause of homosexuality is incest—especially of parents with children. Avoidance of incest is basic to healthy sexual relations and of stable families. Anthropologist Claude Levi-Strauss believes the incest taboo marks the transition points from nature to culture and is thought by many to be more consequential than that against homosexuality. There is a strong movement today to make incest acceptable, and the practice of incest is rapidly growing. Kinsey, in his early studies, claimed one out of sixteen women had experienced an incestuous relationship. Robert L. Geiser, Chief Psychologist at the Nazareth Child Care Center in Boston, now claims that 10% of our population may have known such a relationship. Benjamin DeMott in his article "The Pro-Incest Lobby" says, "The movement to weaken the incest taboo demonstrates the force in our time of a particular sense of self." [57] When a parent uses his or her child for self-gratification, selfishness has reached its extreme limit, and there is little hope for the family or any meaningful social relationships.

Conclusion

All of these trends toward the exaltation of the individual over the family are breaking down the social structure.

Claire Booth Luce has said, "Assuming the present growth rate of crime, alcoholism, drug taking and commercialized sex persists into 1996, America by then will be the most drunken, drug-soaked, sex-ridden, and criminal society on earth. To what can we look to prevent this self-destructive process from ending as it must end—in anarchy?" [58]

We need to face seriously the question: Will American men and women as social creatures lose their humanness and drop to the level of the animals as has happened often before in history? Animals must be controlled and if uncontrolled they must be destroyed. Do we want that?

Part Two

GOD'S CALLING TO MEN AND WOMEN IN THE FAMILY

Chapter 7

THE GENDER OF GOD AND
WHY MAN HAS AUTHORITY

Theologians and Feminists Claim Biblical Support

Betty Friedan, speaking to a rally in New York City on Women's Liberation Day in 1970, said, "I think that the great debate of the 1970's will be 'Is God He?' " Theological interpretations about sex roles have been important from the beginning of the feminist movement in the United States in the early nineteenth century, but now are becoming crucial.

On one hand some theologians have rendered the women's movement as heretical, and on the other some of the feminists and their supporters have claimed biblical data as a ground for their view of "liberation." Lucretia Mott, one of the earliest feminist leaders, joined the liberal Hicksite group of the Quakers and claimed the liberty of the prophetic spirit to loose women from religious prohibitions. These claims have continued until today, the most prominent modern advocate being Ruth Carter Stapleton, the president's sister, through whom President Carter gained a deepening of his born-again experience. Mrs. Stapleton is a committed and capable Christian. Conversely, many of the Bible-believing churches offer perhaps the most formidable lobby against feminism. Since two-thirds of the American people are members of the Christian churches, the teachings of the Bible become very important.

God's Gender and the Roles of Men and Women

The opening chapters of the Bible and the first revealed relationship of God to man and woman are crucial for understanding the whole Bible. The Scripture records that after God created all other plant and animal life He said, "Let us make *man* in *our image,* according to our likeness; and let *them* rule over the fish of the sea and over the birds of the sky and over the cattle and over all the earth, and over every creeping thing that creeps on the earth." "And God created *man in His own image,* in the image of God He created him, *male* and *female* He created *them.* And God blessed *them;* and God said to *them,* Be fruitful and multiply, and fill the earth, and subdue it; and rule . . ." (Genesis 1:26–28a; 5:2).

This Scripture indicates that mankind included both male and female human beings. It also shows that God, which is a masculine plural word in Hebrew, also includes both male and female aspects equally. This shows that godlikeness involves femaleness as well as maleness and that humanity also includes both. Moreover, both the man and woman were given authority to subdue and rule the earth. Therefore, to object to addressing God as masculine or the use of the generic word man, in the sense of mankind, is to fail to appreciate the biblical data. Femaleness is equally presented as being of the divine image, and God identified as fully with the characteristics of the woman. There should therefore be no offense as to what gender is used if both sexes are represented.

The names for God—Elohim (God), Elshaddai (Almighty), Jahweh (Self-existent One), Adonai (Lord), and others—all have masculine endings. All personal pronouns also are masculine—Him, His, Us, etc. Titles, too, such as Lord, King, Prince, Father, et al., are masculine. On the other hand, the word for Spirit is feminine in the Hebrew (ruach) and is neuter in the Greek (ta pneuma), but it always appears with a masculine noun, such as "the Spirit of *God,*" "the Spirit of the *Lord.*" Most important of all, when God became incarnate He chose the form of a man, Jesus Christ. So God generally was revealed as masculine, but the feminine person of the Spirit of God is united in the Trinity.

While God is revealed primarily as male, He also exhibits female characteristics. Those statements are carefully worded to show that the God revealed as male is acting in feminine ways. For example, God says the following: "As one whom his mother comforts, so I will comfort you . . ." (Isaiah 66:12,13); as a mother gives birth, so God will give birth to *His* people, city, etc. (Isaiah 46:3,4; 66:7–14; cf. John 3:3–8). Always the statement is "As . . . so I"; never "I *am* a mother. . . ." The Apostle Paul also claimed to act as a mother begetting and caring for his people, but no one ever accuses Paul of *being* female (cf. 1 Thessalonians 2:7; Galatians 4:19).

Words of feminine gender are used to describe God's actions (e.g., torah, "teaching"; chokmah, "wisdom"; shekinah, "God's presence"; bat kol, "voice"; ruach, "spirit"; rehem, "mercy or compassion"). Most of these words are also used of actions of men, and are no indication the person *is* female. To illustrate God's acts by a woman's actions (e.g., the *woman* looking for a lost coin) does not make God female. In the other two illustrations of the same truth, God's concern is illustrated by a man (a shepherd, a father; cf. Luke 15). But both male and female concepts are involved in describing God's character and actions.

Character qualities often have been identified as male or female. The truth is that all positive character traits are *human* traits which may apply to either men or women, although because of the physiological and psychological differences resulting, some character traits tend to be identified more as masculine and others as feminine. But God identifies with all character traits, and especially in the New Testament seems to exalt the more feminine ones. For example, Jesus wept with compassion (cf. Luke 19:41; John 11:33,35); He was meek and gentle (Matthew 11:29); He was passive and submissive under suffering (1 Peter 2:21–3:2), and so on (cf. Luke 13:34; 18:16, et al.).

God's Role of Authority Assigned to the Man Because of Sin

The Bible opens with an ideal relationship between man and woman. Adam was first created and then Eve. Animals were not adequate as his companion, but the woman, created from his side to be his helper, was. God brought her to Adam and the two were to become one flesh. They were not ashamed or afraid, even though they were naked. While they were commanded to be fruitful and multiply, thus enjoying sexual reproduction, there was no apparent difficulty in doing this. Together they were to keep and expand the garden until they had dominion over the earth. Marriage existed, but no dominion over or submission to the other is mentioned (Genesis 1:26–31; 2:7–25).

The man was identified with the divine gender to designate sequence of origin and beneficial purpose, not because masculinity represented superiority (1 Corinthians 11:8,9; 1 Timothy 2:13). They lived as equals in social harmony, willingly under God's control. Some feel that the woman was created as "a helper" and this implies subservience. The same Hebrew word is used to describe God as "the helper" of Moses' son, Eliezer (Exodus 18:4), which certainly does not imply inferiority of God, but only indicates one who cares and helps. The description of her as a "helper *suitable* (Hebrew means 'corresponding to him')," which could not be said of any animal (Genesis 2:18,20), implies a comparable intelligence that could furnish companionship and prevent his being lonely (Genesis 2:18). The fact that she was made from man indicates she was of the same essence and equal to him (Genesis 2:22,23).

After Eve led Adam into transgression, God established human government for the preservation of the race *until redemption could be completed.* He chose to give that authority to the man (Genesis 3:16) because the woman was first deceived and fell in the transgression and because Adam was first created and the woman was created from him to complement him (Genesis 2:18,20–23; 3:1–6; 1 Timothy 2:13,14; 1 Corinthians 11:8,9). The purpose of God's redemption is to renew His authority or kingdom rule over men and women (Mark 1:15; Titus 2:11–14; Colossians 1:13). So the man, as the one to represent authority for God, needed to be associated with authority until redemption is complete and God's reign over the world is fully established.

Biblically, God's original design was that neither sex would be more identified with authority than the other but that both look to God's authority. Because of sin God temporarily redefined the sex roles for mankind's benefit and for His own glory. The offense today is not because God is identified with maleness but because *maleness is identified with God's authority.* Sinful men and women do not wish to be submissive to the control of another, God or human (cf. Romans 8:7,8). This is the crux of the whole matter! Sin expressed as selfish individualism is the great human problem. The essence of sin is the desire to exalt *self*—to "be like God" (Genesis 3:5).

Because God identified His authority with the man for purposes of temporary human government until His kingdom would be reestablished, to try to feminize God or to remove authority from men weakens the concept of His moral government and is satanic. As mentioned (p. 86), when worship in the Jerusalem temple reached the point of perversion so as to center on female deities, God's kingdom over Judah was terminated and the temple was destroyed by God.

God in His sovereign wisdom chose to identify the male gender with authority. Although the role of authority and leadership is attributed to the man *during the time of the redemptive process,* after redemption is complete following the resurrection of believers, marriage and its responsibilities will be ended. The redeemed will be as the angels, who don't marry (Matthew 22:30). The sinful natures of men and women will have been changed and they all will be united under Christ's rule, the eternal basis for society. So the roles of men and women are limited to the time when they are in the flesh to enable them to be "one flesh," as God originally intended (Genesis 2:24). After the resurrection Christ still will be identified as masculine and authoritative. While each Christian will be recognized by the pre-resurrection gender, the feminine concept will predominate because believers together will be identified as Christ's bride (cf. Ephesians 5:22,23). As His bride, all believers will be gloriously united to Him at the marriage supper of the Lamb (Matthew 22:1–14; 25:10; Revelation 9:7,9; 21:2). Then both men and women will rule with Christ over the world and over angels (1 Corinthians 6:2,3).

Sex Roles Furnish Interdependence to Counteract Sinful Individualism

Establishment of male leadership after the sin of Adam and Eve was necessary because the sin nature resulting from their fall exalted the individual self over against

God and others. They partook of the fruit of the prohibited tree of the knowledge of good and evil. Satan told them if they ate they would become "wise as God, knowing good and evil" (Genesis 3:1 ff). That meant both Adam and Eve would begin to be "wise in their own eyes" and be their own standard-makers, determining what is good and what is evil, what is right and what is wrong (cf. Isaiah 5:20,21). Being "as God," they thought they would no longer need to accept God's word as to what is right and wrong, good or evil.

In innocence, while trusting God, Adam and Eve also trusted and accepted each other as a companion given by God. But in sin man was insecure and cut off from God, so he began seeking his own individual interest over others and over society. After the transgression their sin natures led them to see their naked differences as a threat that caused shame and fear. "Is he better than I?" or, "Is she better than I?" was the question. Shame and fear inevitably breed hate and conflict. Physical differences, whether sex, race, or even a big nose, can become a threat because of our individual insecurity. Adam said, "I was afraid because I was naked" (Genesis 3:7,10).

Fear and hate are the opposite of love and cause barriers between people (1 John 4:18–20). Therefore, to keep them from totally separating from each other and from Him and to preserve the race, God altered the functions of man and woman and made them interdependent until redemption would be accomplished—until the seed of the woman would bruise the head of the seed of the serpent (Genesis 3:15). God cursed the serpent and the earth and changed the roles of man and woman so they would need and desire each other. By increasing the social responsibilities between men and women He helped overcome their sinful individualism. He also covered their nakedness to diminish the offense.

Woman Made Dependent on Her Husband

God did two things to cause the woman to be dependent. The woman's childbearing functions were changed—her conception of children was altered, and her pain in bearing them increased: "I will multiply your *labor* and *conception*" (Hebrew: itsvbownek weheronek; Genesis 3:16, trans. from Hebrew).

There is some evidence in nature which may suggest what God did to increase her conception. God created men to be biologically very similar to the other anthropoid animals. But there are now some striking differences between animals and mankind which suggest how God changed woman's biological functions to cause her to have children more frequently than she would have. Of the anthropoids, only man is continuously fertile. The man constantly has sperm and the woman ovulates monthly, making sex a continuous drive. The woman is continuously sexually stimulated while the anthropoid animals have only periods of heat. Thus the possibility of sexual attraction and conception is constant for the woman, but not for animals. Without the use of contraception the woman may repeatedly conceive.

Dr. Jan Lever, professor of zoology at the Free University at Amsterdam, has pointed out some other interesting differences between man and the higher anthropoids which suggest how woman's labor in bearing and nurturing children was increased. The gestation period of man is longer and the baby born is proportionately much larger. A gorilla may be three times the weight of a woman, yet the woman's offspring is larger—around three kilograms, while the baby gorilla is only two kilograms. It would appear that the development of a human baby has been prolonged by God so it is larger at birth, therefore creating greater pain in pregnancy and in birth.

Dr. Lever also observes that the human fetus seems

to go through a period from the third to the fifth months where it resembles a nest-fleeing animal (e.g., calves, colts, apes). Such animals have few offspring, and their offspring have very little dependence as soon as they are born. Is it possible that the human infant, according to God's original design, would have been born nest-fleeing at four months so that he would have been smaller and easy to deliver and yet less of a responsibility for the mother after birth? It is a fact that the human baby born after nine months is naturally more dependent on the mother and for a longer period of time than almost any higher animal.[1]

Because of the woman's frequency of conception and difficulty in birth and nurture, she *must depend* on her husband to provide for and protect her and their children. God said, "Your desire shall be for your husband, and he shall rule over you" (Genesis 3:16).

Some commentators have suggested the major curse for the woman was bearing sinfully depraved children. While this no doubt is a burden of mothers, it does not fit the Hebrew description of 'labor' and 'conception,' which was to be multiplied.

As we showed in Chapter Three, two things make a man want a woman as a companion and helper: the continuous sexual love she offers and the feeling of importance he has in having her look to him as her leader and provider. These also furnish him a sense of identity.

Natural Evil Requires the Man's Dependence on God

Because a man can be selfishly despotic in regard to his wife, who is physically weaker, God cursed the ground, producing "thorns and thistles," so that man's job of providing is dependent on His blessing (Genesis 3:17–19; 5:29). The word 'thorns' (Hebrew: 'gots') literally means "something that makes one sick or hurts"; and 'thistles' (Hebrew: 'dardar') means "that which flows forth or grows quickly and luxuriantly." Thus new climatic changes would seem to favor the growth of vegetation or insects that would interfere with food production, and natural catastrophies such as earthquakes, floods, and drought would hurt men and cause them to look to God for help. It is God who sends the rain and causes the sun to shine in order that food may be provided (Matthew 5:45). If a man doesn't trust God or mistreats his wife, God withholds His blessing and does not answer prayer to help him to provide (Malachi 3:13–16; 1 Peter 3:7). Thus the man is made dependent on God. The man's leadership of his family in the worship of God becomes primary for the happiness of the family.

Jesus reemphasized mankind's dependence on God when He said, "Seek first His [your heavenly Father's] kingdom and His righteousness; and all these things [food, clothes, etc.] shall be added to you . . . Do not be anxious for your life, as to what you shall eat, or what you shall drink, nor for your body, as to what you shall put on" (Matthew 6:33,25).

To summarize, by the so-called "curses" the woman was made dependent on her husband and the husband dependent on God for his family. A glue of interdependence was added.

Life-Long Marriage to One Person

God intended marriage to be monogamous and lifelong. Jesus made this quite clear and pointed out that divorce was a result of human sin (Matthew 19:3–9). The commandment against adultery was seen as binding in the Old and New Testaments as an expression of love for one's neighbor (Exodus 20:14; Romans 13:9; Matthew 5:27,28). Infidelity was listed by Jesus as a grounds for divorce, probably because the "unity" of marriage has already been abrogated when that occurs (Matthew 5:32; 19:9). Some feel that Paul says the Lord sanctioned divorce when an unbelieving spouse rejects a believer (1 Corinthians 7:10–15).

The law against adultery prohibited marital infidelity and was interpreted to prohibit all forms of sexual perversion. Premarital relations were forbidden in Israel, and those found committing such an act were forced to marry and could never legally be divorced (Deuteronomy 22:29). One act of immorality was enough to cause a woman to be considered a harlot, and the man and the woman were to be punished by stoning (Deuteronomy 22:20,21). Acts of incest, homosexuality, and bestiality also were to be radically punished (Leviticus 18:4–30; 20:10–23). The reason for such harsh treatment is that the prevalence of these sins was a main cause for God's destruction of nations and would lead to the destruction of Israel also (Deuteronomy 8:19,20).

In establishing the New Testament church among all nations, Jesus and His apostles continued to warn against perverse sex acts as wrong, but withheld the harsh civil judgment of stoning (cf. John 8:1–11; Acts 15:20; 1 Corinthians 6:15–18; Galatians 5:19,20; Romans 1:26,27, et al.). But one continuing in such sin without genuine repentance was to be put out of the church (1 Corinthians 5:1–5). Punishment for sin would come at the final judgment at the end of history.

Marriage fidelity is the most basic point for honesty. All other honesty grows out of it. If your partner sees you as disposable at the slightest failure, how can there be trust? Fidelity in life-long monogamous marriage is the way of maximum trust.

Many have tried to support polygamous marriage from Scripture, but an adequate evaluation of the data will not support this. Abram had relations with Hagar, the maid of his wife Sarai, but God had him send her and her child away, with considerable heartbreak to Abraham (Genesis 21:10–12). Jacob was tricked by Laban to take two of his daughters instead of just Rachel, the one he loved. That was not Jacob's original intent. Controversy between his two wives led to his involvement with their two handmaids. The competition, bitterness, and heartbreak that resulted clearly speak against polygamy (Genesis 21, 30, 37). Moses warned the future kings against taking many wives (Deuteronomy 17:17). Saul began with only one wife (1 Samuel 14:50), but he later wanted to be like other kings, so he took several wives (2 Samuel 12:8). This vain desire to please the people also led him into other acts of disobedience for which he was removed from his office by God (1 Samuel 13:14; 15:28; 1 Chronicles 10:13,14).

David began by being married to Saul's daughter Michal. He loved her and was true to her for years until Saul took her and gave her to another man to spite David (cf. 1 Samuel 18:20,28; 19:11,12). David let this cause him to abandon his monogamy, and he took two wives while in the wilderness, Abigail and Ahinoam of Jezreel (1 Samuel 25:42–44). When he became king at Hebron he took other wives. When he became king over all Israel in Jerusalem he took still others. His continued love for Michal is seen in that his one request of the leaders of Judah when he became their king was that they restore Michal as his wife (2 Samuel 3:13,14). David's abandonment of monogamy for the practice of taking any woman he wanted led to his taking Bathsheba, the wife of Uriah, and to his having Uriah killed (2 Samuel 10,11). God sent Nathan the prophet to rebuke David for those sins, and David suffered the death of his son and incest, murder, and armed rebellion by his own children as a judgment for his sin (2 Samuel 12–18). Solomon, his son, continued the practice of polygamy, and it led to his undoing and judgment by God (1 Kings 11:1–13). Therefore, the Scriptures do not seem to approve of polygamy.

Unfortunately, the Mormons, the Church of Jesus Christ of Latter-Day Saints, have influenced many to believe they advocate a high biblical view of the family.[2] However, the history of Mormonism shows their approval of polygamous marriage and even promises a non-biblical concept of polygamous sensuous sexual intercourse in heaven similar to what the Koran teaches. The founding leaders of Mormonism practiced polygamy: Joseph Smith had 28 wives; Brigham Young, 27; J. M. Grant, 5; Ezra T. Benson, 4; P. P. Pratt, 9; etc. Smith claimed the doctrine of plural and celestial marriages was revealed to him from heaven in 1843, and it was published as a principal doctrine of the church, becoming church law in 1852. In 1885 Mormon President Wilford Woodruff declared, "We did not reveal celestial marriage. We cannot withdraw or renounce it. God revealed it, and He has promised to maintain it and to bless those who obey it." Moreover, this view of marriage is consistent with their view of God. Brigham Young taught there are many gods who retain fleshly organs and appetites and who throughout eternity beget children by polygamous marriages.[3]

Equal Importance in the Bible of Both Roles in Redemption

The unfolding of God's redemptive plan and the building of His kingdom centered on the roles of woman's childbearing and nurture and man's leadership and teaching. The redemptive drama hinged on women conceiving and bearing the spiritual seed who would lead God's people (Genesis 3:15). God's miraculous working in the woman was repeatedly the focal point. As a result of prayer He enabled her to conceive when naturally she could not. Some to whom this happened were Sarah, Rebecca, Rachel, Leah, Hannah, the wife of Manoah, the young woman in Isaiah 7:14, Elizabeth, and finally Mary the mother of Jesus.

As previously mentioned (p. 16), Abraham was chosen as father of God's family to teach his children to believe and to walk in God's ways (Genesis 18:18,19). The will of God was to be passed on by the teaching of the father to the son and the grandson in the nation of Israel (Deuteronomy 6:1–7; Psalm 78:5–8; Proverbs 1:8; 3:1; 4:1).

In the New Testament the climax of the male role was in Jesus Christ as King, Teacher, and sacrificial Redeemer. All of Jesus' apostles were men. Paul says a ruling bishop, or elder, and a deacon should be "the husband of one wife" and "one who rules well his household, having his children in subjection" (1 Timothy 3:2–5,12 KJV). He shows that this responsibility of the man to raise his children in the nurture and admonition of the Lord continued from the Old Testament to the New (Ephesians 6:1–4), with the promise of long life to the nation in the land (Deuteronomy 5:33–6:7). The child-bearing emphasis for women and the leadership authority for men are found through the New Testament to the end, where "the seed of the woman" has victory over the seed of the serpent (Revelation 12:5).

Scripture teaches that salvation from the power of Satan or sin (sanctification) is achieved by trusting God in fulfilling these roles. Paul told Timothy, "Pay close attention to yourself and to your teaching; persevere in these things; for as you do this you will insure salvation both for yourself and for those who hear you" (1 Timothy 4:16). He also declares, "Women shall be saved through the bearing of children if they continue in faith and love and sanctity with self restraint" (1 Timothy 2:15). He warns later, "I want younger widows to get married, bear children, keep house, and give the enemy no occasion for reproach; for some have already turned aside to follow Satan" (1 Timothy 5:14,15). By fulfilling the feminine role of producing children and molding them for God, the women thereby gain personal significance (1 Corinthians 11: 11,12), and so avoid Satan's snares. Salvation in these verses does not refer to how one is made acceptable to God and gains deliverance from the guilt of sin. That is by grace alone.

Chapter 8

NEW TESTAMENT SERVANT ROLES AIM AT SOCIAL STABILITY

Submissive Service Produces Social Stability

In the New Testament the roles of the husband and wife are most often listed in the context of other roles that affect social stability. They are most often considered from the point of view of a person in a servant's position who is subject to abuse by one who has authority over him or her. In each passage of Scripture the emphasis is that *individual rights* should be trusted to God and the person should assume the role of a *servant of God for the benefit of society.*

Peter calls Christians to excellent behavior before unbelievers (gentiles) and says, *"Submit yourselves* for the Lord's sake to every human institution." He then reviews some servant roles: citizens to the king and his governors (1 Peter 2:13–17), and servants to masters, even when the master is abusive (2:18–25). Peter then says, "In *the same way,* you wives, be submissive to your own husbands . . ." (3:1–6), and "You husbands *likewise,* live with your wives in an understanding way, as with a weaker vessel, since she is a woman; and grant her honor as a fellow-heir of the grace of life, so that your prayers may not be hindered. To sum up, let *all* be harmonious, sympathetic, brotherly, kind-hearted, and humble in spirit, not returning evil for evil, or insult for insult, but giving a blessing instead" (3:7–9).

Paul's famous statements (which have mistakenly been called a chain of command) begin as do Peter's, and are actually a chain of submission. *"Be subject to one another* in the fear of Christ" (Ephesians 5:21). He then says, *"Wives, be subject* to your own husbands, as to the Lord. For the husband is the head of the wife, as Christ also is the head of the church . . ." (5:22–24). *"Husbands, love* your wives, just as *Christ* also loved the church and *gave Himself up* for her . . ." (5:25–33). *"Children, obey* your parents in the Lord . . . *Fathers . . . bring them up . . ."* (6:1–4). *"Slaves, be obedient* to those who are your masters . . ." (6:5–8). *"Masters, do the same things* to them, and give up threatening, knowing that both their Master and yours is in heaven, and there is no partiality with Him" (6:9; cf. also Colossians 3:18–4:1). Paul and Peter both aim at social stability.

In Galatians Paul gives a different but related emphasis, saying, "You are all sons of God through faith in Christ Jesus. For all of you who were baptized into Christ have clothed yourselves with Christ. There is neither Jew nor Greek, there is neither slave nor free man, there is *neither male nor female;* for you are all one in Christ Jesus" (Galatians 3:26–28). Many use these verses to say that in Christ the roles of distinction are no longer valid, but the next verse removes the possible contradiction with Paul's other statements. It says, "If you belong to Christ, then you are Abraham's offspring, *heirs* according to promise" (3:29). The roles of service exist *now,* to enable sinful people to relate successfully in this temporal world, but in God's eyes there is equal acceptance, and in God's final future kingdom, after the judgment and resurrection, men and women will function equally. They are now *heirs* to equality of function. Peter uses this to motivate husbands to treat their wives with honor: because she is "a *fellow-heir* of the grace of life" (1 Peter 3:7).

Judgment and Future Reward are the Motive

Paul and Peter remind the masters of slaves that they have a Master who will judge them and that slaves belong to Him as well. Hence, future judgment and rewards are a motive to *refrain from abusing* those who are servants now. And from the servant's point of view, service today should be done "in the Lord" and "as unto the Lord," looking toward heavenly reward. Those who truly believe in the resurrection and lordship of Christ can therefore be willing to accept these servants callings, but it is much harder for those who do not.

Christ's suffering as a servant before His persecutors is used as an example of how a woman should willingly suffer abuse from her husband for the Lord, if need be (I Peter 2:21–3:1). Also, the husband is instructed to be an unselfish sacrificial leader of his wife under Christ, "as Christ loved the church and gave Himself up for her" (Ephesians 5:25).

Men's Role and the Christian View of Economics

The husband's call to love his wife as Christ loved the church and gave Himself for it (Ephesians 5:25) involves providing for and protecting her. His role is one of an economic servant as well as a leader. We have seen that in the breakdown of the home the man begins to find his identity and power in wealth that he has selfishly accumulated, and ceases to see that wealth as something for which he is a steward of God.

Abraham is given as an example of a father of faith (Romans 4:11,12, etc.). Abraham did not trust in money or make it an objective or goal. His goal was to have a child whom he would raise for God's glory. God chose him "in order that he may command his children and his household after him to keep the way of the Lord by doing righteousness and justice" (Genesis 18:19). He left his home in Ur and in Padan-aram, trusting God to give him a land. He ultimately looked for a heavenly city, "whose architect and builder is God" (Hebrews 11:10). He therefore did not fight over who got the best business deal, but gave his nephew Lot the first choice (Genesis 13), and he refused to accept the great riches offered by the kings of Sodom and Gomorrah lest it be said that wicked men had made him rich (Genesis 14:21–23). Nevertheless, God blessed Abraham and gave him riches (Genesis 13:2).

Unfortunately many Christians have taught that capitalism is the Christian view of economics. Capitalism teaches that every man has the right to own and pile up as much wealth as he wishes for himself. The emphasis is on the *right* of private ownership. We have shown that greed is idolatry.

The biblical view is that of a stewardship of responsibility to God. God entrusts money and material things to men to use as servants for God's glory (Matthew 25:14–30). A man is to earn money so he may provide for himself (2 Thessalonians 3:10; 1 Thessalonians 4:11,12) and his wife and children in a sacrificially loving way (Ephesians 5:26–33). To fail to do so is to deny the faith and be *"worse than an unbeliever"* (1 Timothy 5:8).

The Bible also emphasizes the man has a responsibility before God to earn more than he needs to be able to help those in the community who have less than he (Ephesians 4:28; Acts 4:34,35). He should share first with the needy in the Christian community and then with unbelievers in need (Galatians 6:10). At times it may involve giving to Christians in need in other areas of the world (1 Corinthians 16:1–4; 2 Corinthians 8, 9). This should be especially directed toward helping children and women who are widows (Acts 6:1–6; James 1:27). Men should also work in order to support those who work hard to preach the gospel and spread the kingdom of God (1 Corinthians 9:1–11; Galatians 6:6,7; Philippians 4:14–19).

The basic rule in economics is to "love your neighbor *as yourself*" (Matthew 22:39). A Christian should want to see others have as much as he has. The man who continually piles up wealth for himself and does not share it to help others is not a Christian in economics. Dives, the rich man who died and went to hell, did not steal or kill. He just was trusting in money and did not care for Lazarus, his neighbor who was in need (Luke 16:19–31). He had been unfaithful with unrighteous mammon and therefore could not be entrusted with true riches (Luke 16:11–13). He is a fool who devotes himself to capitalistic piling up of wealth for selfish security (Luke 12:13–31). It is therefore very difficult for rich men to enter the kingdom of God (Mark 10:17–31). Showing partiality to the rich is a violation of the law of love and is sin (James 2:8,9). Electing wealthy men to offices of the church because they are rich and influential is one way the church has sinned.

There are those today who go to the other extreme in seeking to give government control over all money to distribute it. The early Christians were not communists or socialists. They believed Christ was alive from the dead, and they trusted in Him and ceased to trust in money. So they sold their excess property and gave away the excess money they had (Acts 2:32,44,45; 4:34,35). But they did this voluntarily because the money had been given to them by God (Acts 5:4). They still kept their own private homes, but opened them in hospitality to others (Acts 12:12; Romans 16:5; 1 Corinthians 16:19; Colossians 4:15).

The man's role is therefore to work creatively to express

his love for his own family, for the church, the family of God, for any in need, and for God and His kingdom. He should meet and plan with the church to achieve this end. In so doing he performs the role of a sacrificial servant.

Errors Concerning Servant Social Roles

The church has erred when serving God has been seen only as studying the Bible, going to church and praying. Men serve God by doing creative work as servants of His. The church has also erred in giving prominence and leadership to men who have selfishly amassed great wealth, many neglecting their wives and children in the process. Today many in the church are trusting in their riches, and they are the ones who should be challenged to sell all they have and give to the poor (Mark 10:21,22). Unfortunately, some pastors do not exhibit the law of love, but seek large salaries and plush homes. Success in the ministry is often based on how big and beautiful a church building is. It is hard to feel that this represents Jesus, who once said, "Foxes have holes, and the birds of the air have nests, but the Son of Man has nowhere to lay His head" (Matthew 8:20).

The spirit today that urges individual employees to band together in revolt against abuses by their employers, that urges wives to compete with their husbands and renounce their leadership, and which urges children to rebel against parents who are at times abusive, is a spirit contrary to the New Testament. It puts the individual above society. The New Testament calls a person to have a loving spirit toward the one who offers the abuse, and seeks to remove the abuse by calling the abuser to an account before God and by reminding him of eternal judgment. This is the approach of faith; renunciation or rebellion against authority is the approach of the world.

Sacrificial servant love is the approach God used to change sinful men. Paul and Peter recognized that freedom is better than slavery (cf. 1 Corinthians 7:21), but they knew the best way to remove tyranny in government, in the home, or in the working economy was to confront the tyrant with his accountability to God, by exhibiting it by faith.

Those who say that redemption in Christ removes all authority except that of Christ end up removing the authority of Christ in Scripture too. Scripture says, "The husband is the head of the wife *as Christ also is the head* of the church," and that the wife should "be subject . . . in everything" (Ephesians 5:23,24). To deny the husband's headship is to deny also the headship of Christ. Only by the most extreme verbal gymnastics can one change the obvious meaning. To minimize the control of Christ as King over the church is a very serious heretical teaching. While some men of God have mistakenly taught this, it must be rejected.

Prohibitions for Women Protect Privileges of Men and Women

The biblical teaching consistently forbids women to assume leadership in the church over groups with adult men because this would be a contradiction of the husband's leadership in the family. A woman teaching her husband or ruling over him at church is not likely to be subject to him when she goes home. That requires a reversal in thinking.

Paul says, "Let a woman quietly receive instruction with entire submissiveness. But I do not allow a woman to teach or exercise authority over a man, but to remain quiet. For it was Adam who was first created and then Eve. And it was not Adam who was deceived, but the woman being quite deceived, fell into transgression" (1

Timothy 2:11–14). Many have said Paul was speaking to a particular cultural situation which no longer exists and therefore this teaching does not apply today. However, Paul appeals to creation and the woman's universal representation of Eve in the transgression as a basis for his teaching. Hence, this teaching must be interpreted as having universal validity. Jesus also appealed to the conditions of the creation of Adam and Eve for the rule for life-long monogamous marriage (Matthew 19:4). Few would say He was teaching only for a particular cultural situation. Also, Paul is again clearly defending abiding social structures, because his teaching occurs in the context of urging submission to civil governing authorities (1 Timothy 2:2).

It is often argued that Paul is inconsistent with himself because he says in other Scriptures that women could prophesy. Before examining those passages it should be pointed out that Paul's main objective is, "I do not allow a woman to teach or exercise authority over a man." Protecting home leadership authority is his aim. By preserving that authority he thereby also protects the woman's freedom to bear and nurse children.

Chapter 9

WOMAN'S RELATIONSHIP TO GOD

The Prophetic Gift Does Not Convey a Leadership Teaching Role

Prophetic Experience Is Different from Office of Teacher

Throughout Scripture women were given the gift of prophecy. That gift, more than any other, indicated God's immediate encounter and presence through the Holy Spirit in the woman as well as in the man. The Hebrew word for prophesy (nabhi) means "to flow forth." Hence, the essence of the idea was that an experience with God results in an emotional exhilaration leading to a flowing forth of a description about it. Prophecy is based on a direct experience with God whereby God shows the person something which is then shared with others. A false prophet was one who claimed that God had met with and spoken to him, while in fact he was making up the messages himself (Jeremiah 23:16,21,22; Ezekiel 13:17). Hence, prophecy involved relating information out of a direct encounter. In that encounter the person may have seen a vision or had God speak a message to him which he conveyed to others (cf. Exodus 4:16; 7:1). In the Old Testament God disclosed His sovereignty by foretelling coming events to the prophets.

Scripture indicates that it was a common error to think

that because a person had a prophetic encounter a place of governing authority should be allowed also. In the Old Testament the *prophet* and *teacher* were two different functions (Malachi 2:4–8; 3:11; Jeremiah 18:18). The priests were the *teachers* of God's law and covenant (cf. Ezekiel 23:11). They studied God's revealed law, applied it to life, and offered sacrifices and intercession for those who broke it. Their ministry centered around the Ten Commandments contained in the ark of the covenant in the Holy of Holies of the temple. The temple worship involved offering sacrifices and intercession for the people who had broken the law of God that the priest had taught them.

In the New Testament the gifts of *prophet* and *teacher* are also separate and distinct (Ephesians 4:11; 1 Corinthians 12:28). But with the completion of revelation in Christ, God no longer continued to give verbal revelations. Hence, prophecy in the New Testament more and more focused on three objectives which resulted from the Holy Spirit experiences. They are listed in 1 Corinthians 14:3: "One who prophesies speaks to men for edification and exhortation and consolation." Edification (oikodome) means "to build one up." Exhortation (paraklesis) is a word which means "to go alongside a person as a helper and appeal to him." It might involve giving a judgment of correction. Consolation (paramuthian) means "to come alongside a person and tell him a story that will help him." The idea is that a person who has had an experience with God through the Holy Spirit now comes and shares the truth God has taught him with that person so that it will help affirm, appeal to, or console him (2 Corinthians 1:4).

Again, this is not the same as a person *teaching* what the Scriptures say the will of God is and seeing that the hearers live up to it. One involves an office of authority, the other a ministry of sharing and helping.

While the gift of prophet and teacher were different, they had a relationship to each other. Sometimes the prophetic encounter resulted in a God-given message to rebuke the people and call them back to the law which they had forsaken. At other times God's prophetic encounter served as a sign that an individual was acceptable to God, such as when the Spirit came upon Saul or David (1 Samuel 10:10; 16:13). If a person were otherwise selected for any office—judge, king or priest—it might be a symbol of God's approval of that person. But the gift of prophecy did not in itself convey any office.

To be able to prophesy might be, but was not necessarily, accompanied by an office of leadership. When Moses appointed the seventy leaders to help him judge the people, the Spirit came upon them and they all prophesied, showing God's approval. Two men continued to prophesy after the others had ceased, and Joshua interpreted this as a threat to Moses' leadership. Moses dismissed it as no threat to his leadership by saying, "I would that *all* the Lord's people were prophets . . ." (Numbers 11:24–30).

Later Joel predicted that God would pour out his Spirit on *all flesh* and every believer would prophesy (Joel 2:8). On the day of Pentecost this prediction was fulfilled. Even the lowest "handmaid" and "bondservant," men and women, experienced this (Acts 2:17,18). If *all* Christians experienced the prophetic experience, it could not be a sign distinguishing them as leaders! Everyone truly born of the Spirit had a prophetic encounter. But some have a special gift of service in this regard.

Women Prophets Were Not Official Leaders

In one landmark incident in the Old Testament it was demonstrated that a woman's ability to prophesy did not make her an offical leader. Miriam, the older sister of Moses, had interpreted the fact that she and Aaron had the gift of prophecy to mean that they also had the office of leadership equally with Moses. Because of this challenge to Moses' leadership, God smote her with leprosy until Moses prayed for its removal (Numbers 12). Nothing was done to Aaron, although God was angry with him also.

In the New Testament a similar thing occurred. The women's movement of the Hellenistic world had become strong in Palestine the last century before Christ, and the Jews had reacted in a conservative way, restricting women severely. A court of women was added to Herod's temple which prevented the women from approaching the worship center as they had in the previous temples, which had been designed and revealed by God. Moreover, the synagogues were segregated so that women sat in one section and men in another, a condition that did not exist earlier in Jewish assemblies. Women were restricted by the rabbis from higher study of the Torah, or law. The rabbis said the only calling for women was to marry and have children.

Jewish custom had long been that when a woman married she would always wear a small bandana or veil over her head when she went out in public to symbolize that she was under the authority of her husband and not available for marriage (cf. Talmud, Keth. vii, 6, concerning the meaning of the veil). This was not to cover the face or body as with some Moslems. This was simply a symbol of marriage commitment and the authority of the husband, as was the single wedding ring begun by the Romans and still used today.

When Paul expanded Christianity into the gentile world and taught that women were equally valuable and could experience the prophetic presence of the Holy Spirit and a personal encounter with God, the Jewish women who had been restricted overreacted. As Miriam had interpreted her prophetic encounter with God as an equal right to authority, so did the women of Corinth. They began to remove their veils, renouncing their husbands' authority, and prophesy with their heads uncovered (1 Corinthians 11:5). They also did this when they were praying (1 Corinthians 11:13). This renunciation of their husbands' authority was an offense to the protective angels of God (1 Corinthians 11:10).

Paul relates the prevalent custom of women having long hair to this. The hair of a woman is her glory and she usually uses its beauty to attract and win her husband. When a woman was divorced her marriage covenant to her husband ended, and if she was to be married to another, her head was to be shaved. When women were taken in battle, when their husbands were killed, and they were given in marriage to others, their heads were to be shaved (Deuteronomy 20:14; 21:12). The breaking of a single man's Nazarite vow to God also involved shaving the head (Numbers 6:28). When any vow was violated and a new one made, the head was shaved. Paul says if a woman removes her veil or head covering, as if renouncing her vow and her husband's authority, she might as well shave her head. Paul is saying that women may prophesy or pray in a public meeting as long as it is in a way which shows respect for male authority (1 Corinthians 11:5,6,10).

Some expositors, unaware of the Talmudic meaning for the veil, have said Paul was trying to keep the Christian women of Corinth from being identified with the thousands of temple prostitutes in Corinth by urging them to wear veils. The fact is that the ancient city of Corinth that had the temple prostitution was destroyed in 146 B.C., nearly 200 years before Paul wrote, and this had nothing to do with the veils.

Combined Teacher-Prophet Ministry
Was Restricted to Men

At times in the Old Testament God combined the gifts of prophecy and teaching together in certain men. Isaiah, Jeremiah, and Ezekiel were all teaching priests who also had the gift of prophecy. Some other men who were not priests also were called as prophet-teachers.

There are no clear incidences of this being true for a woman. Hulda is the only prophetess who might be put in this category. But Hulda did not take it upon herself to go and rebuke the king and the people. She only shared the message God had revealed to her when she was asked for an interpretation by the king and other official leaders (2 Kings 22:8–20; 2 Chronicles 34:14–28). While Barak asked the prophetess Deborah to accompany him as a leader of the army in the time of the judges, she warned him that if he did not go alone *without her* he would be disgraced by the fact that a woman would be given the victory over Sisera, the enemy leader. And in fact Jael, Heber's wife, was the one who killed the enemy, as Deborah predicted. Deborah was inquired of by men for advice from God at that time and then shared what God told her. The context of events shows this was a time of failing and weak male leadership (see Judges 4, 5). Nowhere in the Old or New Testaments does God give approval to the idea of women being official leaders to teach and enforce His law over men. In times of social decay when women and youth became the leaders, the idea of women acting like men was condemned by God as evil (Isaiah 3:11–13).

Women Were Considered Equally Valuable Before God

Women Have Direct Communion with God

It is important to maintain that women have the gift of prophecy and the right to pray to God in public, since these two experiences show the acceptance of all individuals by God in the New Testament. But it is wrong to equate prophecy with preaching and conclude that women should also be official teaching elders. Today I believe it would be proper to invite women to speak in church and share truth God is showing them and to call on godly women to pray in public. Evangelical churches today are failing to do this and are not giving women the recognition of their equal value before God. This could open the door for Satan to bring feminism into the church.

Some may appeal to Paul's statement in 1 Corinthians 14:34, "Let the women keep silent in the churches, for they are not permitted to speak," and reject women's public participation. But in interpreting this teaching it must be remembered that Paul has already said that women can prophesy and pray in public (chapter 11). However, it also should be remembered that the women of Corinth were doing this in a disorderly and rebellious way. Paul was concerned about doing everything so that it was edifying (14:26) and in decent order (14:40). In the verses, 14:26–40, he uses the construction "Let . . .", indicating a command, seven times. It seems therefore that he is telling the elders how to moderate the meeting so it is orderly. He is saying that the women should be quiet and not speak out on their own or even try to gain the floor by asking questions. But this does not mean they can't prophesy, pray, or speak in tongues when called upon by the presiding elder and when it is done according to the way Paul previously described. This interpretation seems to be in harmony with the recognition of woman's equal value and also with the recognition of the roles of men and women.

Women's Equal Ability to Perceive and Experience Truth

Not only does the Bible teach women were created

equally in the image of God and are joint heirs to eternal life, but they also were given equal opportunity to understand, experience and share the truth. Mary of Bethany was given the opportunity to be in Jesus' discipleship group and "sit at His feet" to learn (Luke 10:38–42; cf. Paul, Acts 22:3). Mary alone discerned that Jesus would be crucified (Mark 14:8). To Martha Jesus gave the teaching that He was the resurrection and the life (John 11:25,26). It was to the women that Jesus first disclosed He was alive from the dead and instructed them to go tell His male disciples to meet Him in Galilee (Matthew 28:9,10), where He gave the great commission to go and proclaim the gospel to all nations. Since only men were officially commissioned as apostles to go proclaim the gospel, Paul only mentions the men who saw Jesus alive and "proclaimed" it (1 Corinthians 15:3–11), omitting the women's experiences.

Women Can Minister Too

A group of women traveled with Jesus, as did the twelve (Luke 8:1–3), and probably ministered to the women who came to Him, as well as helping Jesus and His apostles by serving them. Paul mentions Phoebe, a servant (deaconess) of the church of Cenchrea, and some feel he sees a servant office for women (Romans 16:1; 1 Timothy 3:11). But no such office appears in the writings of the earliest church fathers. Paul tells of older women who were to teach the younger women in the practical areas of helping their husbands (Titus 2:3–5). Women were to help their husbands in teaching their sons and daughters the truth of God (Proverbs 1:8; 6:20, et al.; 2 Timothy 1:5).

In Israel a boy became a responsible adult at twenty years of age (Numbers 14:29; Exodus 30:14; 38:26; Numbers 13, et al.), and from that time he was considered answerable to God for his own actions. Presumably, there-fore, the age of twenty is the time when women would cease to teach men. But even after that a mother's words would be considered valuable counsel.

Paul had women who helped him in his ministry, al-though in what capacity is not clear (Romans 16:1,3,6; Philippians 4:2,3). Priscilla, with her husband Aquila, "placed before" (Greek-ektithemi, "to place in front of") Apollos a clearer understanding of the truth, helping him to move from the preaching of John the Baptist to the gospel of Christ. To use this reference to make Priscilla an official church teacher with oversight as an elder is to strain the meaning. Every woman of the church who is having a prophetic experience and being taught the Word by the Holy Spirit ought to be personally sharing her understanding with her husband and others to their profit. Some will have the special gift to do this far more capably than others (Acts 21:9). This is necessary to fulfill her role in assisting her husband in the family and in making her contribution to the church.

Most Vocations are Proper for Women

The Christian woman's normal role was to be a wife and mother, but she was to exercise her gifts with great freedom in so doing. There is no biblical reason why a woman should not work in any area she can to help her husband care for their family. All reputable vocations should be open to her. The woman who is entitled "an excellent wife" (Proverbs 31:10–31) weaves cloth and sews it into clothes and sells both. She engages in real estate purchase and sales, makes linen garments and belts and sells them, raises a vineyard, and engages in welfare work. But she does not do these things for her self-gain or glory but for her husband, children and household. Her hus-band is an honored judge and leader of the people because of her help (31:23). "Her children rise up and bless her; her husband also, and he praises her. . . ." (31:28,29).

New Testament women worked in many vocations. The Apostle Paul's first convert in Asia was Lydia, a seller of purple-dyed garments. Priscilla was engaged in tent-making with her husband Aquila.

Paul held a liberal view of women, for a Jew. He broke with rabbinical tradition that said only the father established the sanctity of the family before God, and taught that if the wife was a believer and the husband was not, she could sanctify the home (1 Corinthians 7:14). Paul also held that a woman could serve Christ as a single woman, which demonstrated her independent equal value in the eyes of God (7:34). The rabbis insisted that all women should marry. They were very critical of Paul for his liberal views concerning women (A. Cohen, *Everyman's Talmud,* pp. 179,180).

Women should be able to enter any vocation they can perform well, but as much as we dislike the idea, women on the average will never earn as much as men. In physical jobs women cannot do as much as men. If married women have the children they should, they will cause an added expense in training new workers when they are out. When women can perform equal to men without expense, they should be paid equally. But in liberated America women on the average make only 60 percent of what men make. This is the exact valuation that God gives in the Bible for men to women (50 shekels to 30, Leviticus 27:3,4).

Chapter 10

GOD'S REDEMPTIVE PURPOSES IN NEW TESTAMENT MARRIAGE ROLES

Intimacy and Rough Edges

Marriage brings two people into the most intimate relationship possible, with the parent/child relationship perhaps next. In those close relationships the rough selfish aspects of our personalities become revealed. A wooden board may appear smooth from a distance, but when a good carpenter runs his hand along it, he discovers where it needs sanding. Marriage and family relationships bring us into close contact and reveal rough spots and can furnish the sanding experiences to smooth out our character and demonstrate the love of Christ.

There are *natural reasons* for developing affection between human beings. These can make the marriage meaningful for all people. Homemaking and bearing and nurturing children by the woman, and provision, protection and kind leadership by the man can contribute a basis for caring. Sexual appeal furnishes "eros," self-enjoyment, that attracts. The mutual help, working together, interdependence, allegiance of genetic ties and respect can produce "phileo," or family love, that will hold people together.

Sacrificial Love and Your Family

However, a greater love of man and wife can come through understanding God's plan in the New Testament. Only when two people see God's great love in sending His Son to die on the cross to offer forgiveness will they desire to serve each other submissively in their assigned roles *"for His sake."* Moreover, Jesus Christ has sent His Holy Spirit into people's hearts to grant His men or women the power to accept wrong so that His sacrificial "agape" love can be seen. Christian marriage can have great difficulties, as do others, but it has motivating power to love with Christ's love until the rough edges are made smooth. By the Spirit "the love of God has been poured out within our hearts" (Romans 5:5). "God abides in us, and *His love* is perfected in us" (1 John 4:12). This servant love enables a woman to submit to her husband, even if he is abusive. It also gives the husband the ability to love his wife sacrificially, seek to understand her and put her first—giving himself for her, even if she is not respectful.

Both of these servant roles, voluntarily assumed, witness to the love of Christ in Calvary and prepare the minds of the children to understand the love of God. Instead of grumbling and disputing, Christian couples become lights to a wicked world of people who put their selfish individual rights above care for others (Philippians 2:14,15).

The Cross Removes Selfish Individualism

The problem of selfish individualism can best be solved in the cross of Jesus Christ. When a person believes that Jesus Christ died for him that he might be forgiven and accepted by God, he needs to understand that he was crucified with Christ in the eyes of God. In love for Christ, who now lives for him, he should die to his own desires and be a servant for God to others. God can then enable him to live by the power of the Holy Spirit for others. As we lose our lives for Him we will save them (Galatians 2:20; Romans 6:5–14; 2 Corinthians 5:14–17).

In a community of people who relate to each other as servants for social good, selfish individualism can be dispelled. The church thereby becomes the answer to society. Unfortunately, the church does not usually function this way today.

You may have a fair marriage if you respond to the natural reasons for accepting your spouse. But more and more people are finding that the pressures of individualism and of worldly values cause them to choose to divorce. There is added help for your marriage to make life together more meaningful. If you and your partner will accept Christ's love and accept your role within the family, you will discover deeper joys of love than could ever be experienced in any other way.

In addition, you will begin to promote the kingdom of God through your family and so glorify Him. Moses said that obedience to God's laws should be learned within the home—father to son to grandson—and that the family was the place to apply truth and to train in obedience wherever and whenever there was need (Exodus 20:12; Deuteronomy 5; 6:1–10). Paul referred to Moses' command and promise as the plan of God for *applying* truth today (Ephesians 1:1–3).

Mercy and Compassion for the Repentant and Hurt

While the Bible teaches God's standard is life-long monogamous marriage (Matthew 19:3–9) and the church needs to restore and uphold that standard, there also must be mercy and compassion for those who have failed, who are hurt, and who have genuinely repented (John

8:1–11; Matthew 9:13). In a certain sense there are no innocent parties, in that all parties usually fail in some way, but in another sense there is a guilty party. When a person gives up, drives the other away, forsakes the other, or breaks the marriage bond by infidelity, he or she becomes guilty of violating the marriage covenant (cf. pp. 144, 145; Matthew 5:32; 19:9; 1 Corinthians 7:10–16).

Today there is a tendency of some to swing the pendulum so far toward upholding the life-long monogamous standard that any remarriage of divorced people is prohibited, even in cases of infidelity. Such a position will tend to generate more immorality, and place an undue burden on repentant Christians to whom God has not given the gift of sexual abstinence.

Many people have been deeply hurt by their parents or by another person of the opposite sex. The love of Christ and of the Christian community can help them find healing, even if they have become fornicators, adulterous people, or homosexuals (1 Corinthians 6:9–11). But many of these people will react to their partners in marriage. Many a woman has a negative view of her father and reacts to her husband because of it, and many a man comes from a home with a competitive domineering mother and has deep insecurities which make it difficult for him to be a patient and loving leader. Sometimes both partners have conflicting patterns of reaction which cause great difficulties in marriage. These multitudes of people will need counseling and discipling by Christian leaders to correct these habitual attitudes in order to achieve marriage harmony and servant roles. To teach the Christian ideals of marriage and about God's love will not be enough for them to have victory. They will need encouragement, exhortation, rebuke and oversight from church leaders. But with God's help through the church, any marriage problem can be solved.

The church should show compassion to all who repent of homosexual conduct or immorality. In many cases prolonged counseling and support by the body of Christians may be needed to help the person practice consistent obedience.

The Interrelationship of the Church and the Family

The teaching of the men in the church was to be the model for training the father to lead his home. Paul preached "publicly and *from house to house*" (Acts 20:20). He was "exhorting and encouraging and imploring each one . . . *as a father* would his own children" (1 Thessalonians 2:11). John treated his disciples as "my children" (3 John 4, et al.). We pointed out that the early churches were basically home churches, where the pastor or elders knew and applied the truth to daily life (Romans 16:5; 1 Corinthians 16:19; Colossians 4:25; Acts 10:24, et al.) and the fathers had a model for applying the truth in the family life. The elders of the church gave oversight to families as well as to individuals (Hebrews 13:7,17; 1 Thessalonians 5:12,13). The leaders of the church were chosen on the basis of their effective leadership in the home (1 Timothy 3:4,12; Titus 1:6).

The crisis in many churches lies in the fact that they are weak in the area of human relationships that make possible *specific* application. If a father has a close relationship with his son, correction produces *response*, but if not it produces *reaction*. Some pastors throw the truth out to the crowd attending on Sunday mornings but usually have little opportunity to display specific personal example in life, and no application is made because they seldom relate to the people on a personal basis. Children are sent to Sunday school, where teachers may hardly know their names, much less the needs for application of the lesson truths. Many parents feel they have done their duty by exposing their children to a Christian education in the church, and little or no effort is made to apply Christian teaching at home.

The real issue today in regard to truth is not philosophical. The "battle for the Bible" is only partly in the view of Scripture one holds. One may say he believes the Bible to be inspired, but if he does not obey it and trust and love God and others, the world will not be impressed (John 13:34,35). Unfortunately, Christian families are becoming more and more separated, conflicting, and hurting, like the families of non-Christians. Even outstanding evangelical authors, seminary professors, prominent pastors and other leaders are failing in their families and continuing as leaders without question or discipline. This ought not to be, and God will not let it continue long without judgment. Unless the church returns to the family and the model of it in small home groups that relate, it will soon lose the respect of the people, and no one will take its doctrine seriously.

There are two things that insure the continuation of the church from one generation to another. They are godly women bearing, nurturing, and helping train children, and godly men teaching the Word of God and leading the family and church in application for obedience to it. The church is in danger because both of these are being forsaken by many today.

Chapter 11

SUMMARY OF BIBLICAL TEACHING ON SEX ROLES

Summary

By way of summary, the following diagrams may help show the progressive view of the Bible in regard to sex roles.

1. *At creation,* the following situation existed:

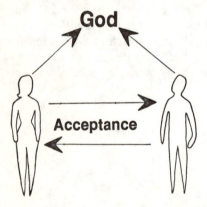

Unity from trust in God

Both the man and woman accepted each other as a companion given from God. She was made from his body, in the image of God, to help him gain dominion over the earth. Hence, society or togetherness existed.

2. *After sin,* this was the situation:

God

Guilt like a cloud

"I'm wise as God"

"I'm wise as God."

Fear for self | Hate | Fear for self

**Self-centered individuals
threatened by the other.**

Sin separated Adam and Eve from God like a thick cloud. Feeling inadequate and trusting only in themselves, fear for their security led to the possibility of a wall of hate to divide them.

3. *After the curses,* natural forces toward family unity:

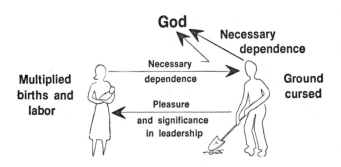

God

**Necessary
dependence**

Necessary
dependence

**Multiplied
births and
labor**

**Ground
cursed**

Pleasure
and significance
in leadership

The result was modified individualism or conditioned unity because of changes in natural conditions. The woman was forced to depend on her husband and on God to restrain him and help her. The husband was forced to depend on God to provide.

By the use of birth control, women can escape this dependence on their husbands. By the use of slave labor (as in ancient Greece or Rome), by oppression of the lower classes by the rich as in some cases, or by use of mechanical or technological machines (as in the modern Western world), men can gain and store up wealth so they can escape or remove the need for prayerful dependence on God to overcome nature. But when the man decreases his dependence on God, and the woman decreases her dependence on the man, selfish individualism, with all its evil, becomes a major threat.

4. In Christ, *during the church age:*

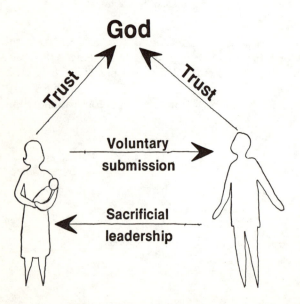

The love of God expressed in the cross and God's power demonstrated in the resurrection enable the husband and wife to trust in God and willingly accept their servant roles of dependence as joint heirs "in the Lord Jesus Christ." Hence, even with contraception and machine technology, men and women can voluntarily and joyfully commit themselves to obey God and use those things to help them fulfill their roles better.

Unfortunately, the relationships of the servant roles are often interpreted as being like diagram A below. A proper interpretaion will show that it should be seen as in diagram B. There the wife is directly under God and places herself voluntarily under her husband for Christ's sake.

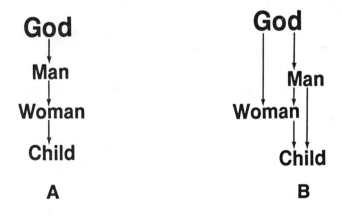

5. *After the resurrection* of believers and the marriage supper of the Lamb:

God the Father, Son (Groom), and Spirit

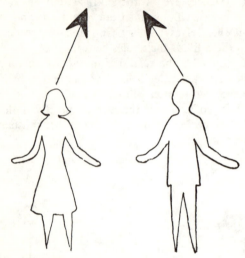

Neither male nor female distinctions or roles will abide. No human marriage or offspring will exist, for all are the bride of Christ. Men and women will rule over the world and angels with Christ.

Conclusions

The Bible recognizes that men and women were created equal in value before God. However, it takes sin seriously and recognizes that without different dependent roles for the sexes to make marriage meaningful, selfish individualism would destroy the family and all society that is produced from the family. Therefore, interdependence within the family relationship was established to secure the well-being of the human race.

Christ's love, in his sacrificial death, becomes the model of servant love which the wife shows in her willing, more passive and submissive obedience to her husband, and the model which the husband demonstrates in his unselfish giving for his wife and children as their leader. Thus the abuses of perverting the roles are minimized.

Also, women can use contraceptives prayerfully so they can better space and care for their children. The men can work hard and prayerfully use machines and technology so they can better provide for their families and give more freely to help people in need and to the building of the kingdom of God. The wife and husband accept these roles for Christ's sake, knowing that there is a glorious future time when they will give an account of their service and be rewarded in an eternal society when both are united as neither male nor female, but as the bride of Christ. But now, until the resurrection, the witness of the kingdom of God through the servant roles in the family is essential. As God's servants, men will be stewards and guardians of creation, not exploiting it for individual personal greed.

The crux of the whole matter is that men and women know and believe in the living God as revealed in Jesus Christ so that they become God's servants to show His love within the home. If men, especially, voluntarily submit to the Lord in giving themselves for their family, the wife and children will likely follow. There is a desperate need today for men who have forsaken the idolatry of pursuing wealth and success and have a passion to know God and follow Him.

We need men like Abraham, who went out of his home country in faith, claiming only God as his shield and reward, obeying, and being God's friend (Genesis 12:1 ff.; 15:1 ff.; Isaiah 41:8), or like Moses, who had a passion to know God in all His glory (Exodus 33:18), or like David, whose heart yearned for God as a deer desires the water brook (Psalm 42:1), or like the Apostle Paul, who said, "I count all things to be loss in view of the surpassing value of knowing Christ Jesus my Lord, for whom I have suffered the loss of all things, and count them but rubbish in order that I may gain Christ" (Philippians 3:8).

Chapter 12

THE DECAY OF NATIONS

The Christian's Concern for His Nation

The Bible devotes more space to the subject of the decay of society in nations than most other topics. Much is said about how this occurs. Space will not allow more than to show the clear course of decay which Scripture draws. But chapter after chapter in the historical books, the prophets, and the Psalms deal with this, and to some extent we find it in the New Testament.

It is important to point out that in the New Testament church the emphasis is on building the kingdom of God made up of people from all nations. Men of all nations are now being brought by faith into submission to Christ, who reigns in heaven. But one day Christ will return in power and great glory to establish His kingdom visibly and judge all nations in a final way.

The Christian belongs to two worlds. He is a citizen of heaven (Philippians 3:20), taking orders from Christ through His word revealed in the Old and New Testaments (2 Timothy 3:16), and he looks forward to the time after his bodily resurrection when that kingdom will be openly triumphant over all other kingdoms (Revelation 11:15–18). That has first priority. At the same time he recognizes that human government has a temporary function for God in the world, which is to restrain evil men and to protect and reward the righteous (Romans 13:1–

7). But the spirit of antichrist is at work in human government, whereby men seek to exalt themselves above the place of God for control of power and wealth over men (1 John 2:15–18; Revelation 13). When earthly rulers cease to perform the function of protecting the righteous and punishing the wicked, they will be judged by God. When an evil ruler gains power in a nation, it is often because the nation has been greedy for the things the ruler promises. In turn, evil rulers lead men toward greater lusts. God is concerned about each individual nation and its response to His laws and His forgiveness through Christ.

The Course of National Decay According to Scripture

The Apostle Paul clearly traces the course of sin among the nations, or gentiles ("gentiles" is the word for "nations" in Greek). Paul reflected over the course of sin in the Hellenistic world in which he lived, and therefore he was looking at the decline of the Greeks and Romans (Romans 1:14,15). In Romans 1:16–2:3 he gives his message. He begins by affirming that the good news of God in Christ is the answer to those who believe (1:16,17). He then outlines the decline as follows:

1. *Men turn from God to idolatry* (1:18–25). Having been prospered by God, they are ungrateful, and being supplied with their needs they foolishly turn from worshiping Him to worshiping the material world He created. The motive behind *idolatry is greed, or covetousness* (Colossians 3:5).
2. *Women and men change their natural use* or role and sex-lust dominates, causing all kinds of immorality, including homosexuality. Perversion of roles leads to breakdown of the home (1:26,27).
3. *Anarchy results from rejection of God and parental control* (1:28,31).
4. *Death from God's judgment comes* (1:32–2:3).

In the first part of this book I have shown that this description of Paul was the pattern verified in the history of Greece and Rome. While each nation developed different cultural emphases and different forms of government, these successive waves of decay were at work, each overlapping the other and growing in intensity. As this is also the pattern developing in America, we must either stem the tide through revival or be judged by God.

God's concern about the conduct of the nations and His judgment of them continue into the age of the New Testament church. It should be remembered that Jesus predicted the judgment of God on Jerusalem and Israel for their sins. This was fulfilled in the years that followed, with the sword of judgment being the Roman armies, in 70 A.D. by Titus, and in 135 A.D. (Matthew 24:1,2). Other passages show the accountability of the various nations to God (Matthew 25:32; Revelation 11:18).

In the Old Testament these steps of decay are clearly laid down. The first *society in Eden* collapsed this way (Genesis 3,4):

1. There was idolatry—Man ceased trusting God the Creator and chose rather to worship the creation (the tree of the knowledge of good and evil) (Genesis 3:1–6).
2. Sexual differences caused offense (3:7–11).
3. Their children committed violence (4:1–8).

In the *times of Noah and Lot* the same elements led to God's judgment (cf. Luke 17:26–30; Matthew 24:37–39; I Peter 3:20; Jude 7; Genesis 6:2,11–13):

1. There was idolatry—They were preoccupied with business and pleasure and were indifferent to God's commands.
2. There were sexual perversions and promiscuity (cf. "took wives for themselves, whomever they chose," Genesis 6:2).
3. There was violence.

The *nations of Israel and Judah* turned to idolatry, then committed gross sexual sins and condoned divorce, which led to much criminal violence. They pursued wealth in their Baal worship (Amos 3:13–15; Isaiah 2:7,8; 5:8; Jeremiah 5:27,28; 6:13, et al.). The women asserted themselves into leadership, sexual promiscuity became prevalent, and marriages broke up (Isaiah 3:12,16; Hosea 4:14; 7:4–6; Jeremiah 2:33; 3:1; 5:8, et al.). Children were unloved and fed to the fires of Molech. Children disobeyed and violence began to prevail. The whole nation was disobedient to God, as many children were to their parents (Jeremiah 2:30; Isaiah 1:2–4; 3:4; 30:1; Hosea 4:1–3; 12:1).

In the Old Testament Moses warned Israel that when God made them rich, if they forgot that He had given them the wealth and began to think that they had gotten it themselves, then the pursuit of wealth would corrupt them and they would be judged by God and destroyed like the decadent Canaanites that God had used them to destroy (Deuteronomy 8). This was what finally brought divine judgment to Israel (Hosea 13:6–8).

Jesus presented mammon worship as the source of the problem. He said, "If therefore your eye is clear [fixed on God], your whole body will be full of light. But if your eye is bad [fixed on mammon], your *whole* body will be full of darkness" (Matthew 6:22,23; cf. Proverbs 28:22). The Apostle Paul said, "The love of money is the *root of all evil*" (K.J.V., 1 Timothy 6:9,10). The Bible nowhere presents money or material wealth as evil, but the love of it and trust in it are evil. God is the Creator of the world, and it is good in itself (Genesis 1:31). In Chapter Three, pp. 43–46, Chapter Four, pp. 53–56, 60, 63, and Chapter Five, pp. 80, 82, we have shown that the sin of greed deceives the man and leads him to free himself from a feeling of the need of submission to woman's monogamous desire and to commit adultery.

The Bible indicates that history is moving toward a consummation, when the principles of evil at work in the world will result in an antichrist worldwide dictator (Daniel 11; 2 Thessalonians 2; Revelation 12,13). The spirit of antichrist is already at work in the world (1 John 2:18; 4:3).

The antichrist will exalt himself and reject all gods (Daniel 11:36; 2 Thessalonians 2:4). He will show no regard for "the desire of women," namely, the desire to bear children (Daniel 11:37). He will control all men so that they cannot buy or sell unless they have the mark of the beast engraved on their foreheads or on their hands (Revelation 13:17). Babylon, the city of idolatrous greed, rides upon this antichrist beast (Revelation 17:7; 18:14–18). One of the best interpretations of the meaning of the number of the beast, 666, is found in 1 Kings 10:14. It was the amount of daily income of Solomon as the richest man in the world. The antichrist will be the leader of the world in wealth, and the world's greatest idolater.

The picture is one of the ultimate exaltation of the individual against God—of one man who is in such control of the world that the sexual distinctives that produce society are subdued to his wishes. He controls the world of creative work and wealth and he denies the childbearing function of women. Perhaps here is a society where women are removed from childbearing, where personal genetic numbers are used for control as recommended by Nobel laureate Linus Pauling (cf. p. 117).

In summary, the biblical teachings agree with the evidence shown in the first part of this book. The forsaking of God by the man to pursue material wealth is seen as the first step toward national decay. This brings about change in the roles consistently maintained in the Bible for both sexes, and that in turn leads to the collapse of the family, producing anarchy and death.

Chapter 13

MORAL DECAY AND A BIBLICAL WARNING

Divine Warning of Coming Grief

The nation of Judah was repeatedly warned by God about the end of its sins, but it was unresponsive. Its greed and lust finally brought it to anarchy. The last kings could hold power only a short time. Then the sovereign God sent Nebuchadnezzar of Babylon to destroy the nation. The great and happy nation of Judah became a place of ruin.

Jeremiah's Lamentations for the nation describe the tragic events: "The joy of our hearts has ended; *our dance has turned to death.* Our glory is gone. The crown is fallen from our head. Woe upon us for our sins" (Lamentations 5:15,16, Tyndale translation).

God's message to all the nations is, "If they will not listen, then I will uproot that nation, uproot and destroy it, declares the Lord" (Jeremiah 12:17). The record of Bible history reveals the fulfillment of this principle. God used the Israelites to destroy the Canaanites, the Assyrians to judge Israel, the Babylonians to judge Judah, the Persians to judge the Babylonians, and so on with many others.

A Divine Sword of Death for America?

Will the great nation of the United States follow this route of sin to ruin and destruction? Many do not believe so. But the people of Judah and most other nations did not believe it would happen to them either. Is there evidence this might happen to America? What nation would God use to destroy America? Surely not the godless nation of Russia that endorses lying and killing as national policy! But many in Judah said the same about Nebuchadnezzar and pagan Babylon in their time (cf. Habakkuk 2:12,13).

The course America is taking is clearly the same as seen in other nations which have gone down to ruin. Moreover, in the very years greed and lust have been growing and undermining the American family, the Soviet Union has risen to superior military power over the United States. Also, while Russia is professedly atheistic, the government of the Soviet Union has enforced some of the moral laws of God as evidenced in nature, even though they haven't acknowledged that these laws were His. Russia has less greed and a higher sexual morality among its people than exists in the United States. God may use Russia as His sword against America.

Can the Russian people really be more moral than America? How could this happen? When Dr. Billy Graham returned from a visit to Moscow a few years ago, he expressed surprise at finding less greed and lust there than in the cities of the United States. There is very little divorce in the Soviet Union, and the crime rate is low. Bronfenbrenner has observed that Moscow and other Russian cities are safe at night for women and children, while New York and other American cities are not.[1] The problem of alcohol and drug abuse is much less than in the United States. These problems are beginning to grow, but they have not reached the threatening proportions that they have in the United States. Why?

The Russian Communists flagrantly violated God's ethical laws to the extreme in the early days of their power. Having experienced the bitter consequences, they have turned back to respect for the family and, without acknowledging Him, to keep some of His laws. Russia under the czars had become very materialistic and lustful. The last of the nineteenth century had given rise to a middle class and more democracy in government. The materialistic Marxist system expressed the desired values for the people, especially the intelligentsia. The society had become unstable, giving the Communists the opportunity to take control.

When the Communists took over Russia in 1917, they almost immediately and fully implemented Karl Marx's teachings. Marx saw the family as a bourgeois institution that was a cause of capitalism. The Communist government under Lenin gave women almost complete freedom from home requirements and allowed divorce by one partner's registering with authorities. Ralph Barnes said in the *New York Herald Tribune* of October 22, 1934, "Divorce in Russia is easier than buying a railroad ticket because it doesn't cost so much." Soon there were more divorces in Moscow than marriages. The result was a rapid breakdown of marriage and morality, and within a few short years (in the 1920's and 1930's) gangs of several million youth—illegitimate and rejected children—roamed the streets and countrysides, stealing, pillaging, and killing. It soon became evident that social order was in jeopardy. Sorokin points out that the whole decay of society occurred under a single regime, and authorities quickly saw that it was unworkable.[2]

When Stalin came to power he used his iron fist to restore the family to dignity. On May 8, 1935, he announced, "The existence of the family must be recognized and provided for." He and the Communist Party made divorce almost impossible, and immorality was looked upon with disfavor. A. S. Makarenko and a dedicated staff were assigned to bring about a pattern of mutual trust and cooperation among the children.[3] Family life was restored. An Associated Press release on November 29, 1935, summarized the initial measures that began to be enacted.

Since the Communists did not like to leave much record of their mistakes, the next generation in the 1960's began an almost complete communization of the family, reducing parental contact with children to a minimum. This brought a reaction from the people and outspokenness by Soviet educators and psychologists in favor of the importance of family love. However, again the ambitions of young Soviet men and women are weakening the family. Parental neglect and discord and conflict in families are beginning to develop.[4]

Because of the military ambition of Soviet leaders, military spending has had priority over consumer goods and desires. Nationalistic purposes have been exalted over personal greed. Russia today spends far more of its gross national income on defense than does America. Hence, their government policy has kept the greed of the men within very restricted limits.

Sex for procreating children is considered important and motherhood is exalted in Russia. The government has established these gradations of honor for mothers:

Mother Heroine Order—Ten or more children. Only about 240,000 women hold this distinction.

Motherhood Glory Order—Seven to nine children. This honor is held by 4.1 million women.

Medal of Motherhood—Five to six children.

There is a cash award for each child from the third on. When there are four children or more, the mother receives a monthly allowance. If she has five children or more, she may retire from work at fifty years of age instead of fifty-five. The Soviets have a birth rate of 18 per 1,000, compared to only 15 per 1,000 in the United States.[5]

The Russians have two levels of responsibility for children. The parents have the primary responsibility, but every citizen is by law required to help care for any children in need or requiring discipline. The state has a strict communal system of nurseries and schools that train children to conform to adult social standards.

Today the family in Russia is reasonably stable and is the source of much honesty and love. Russian schools emphasize putting the rights of the individual second to team responsibility. Russian athletic teams have beaten many others in the world because individuals do not play for their own recognition. The Soviet Union has an amazing record of growth and development. Granted, it has forcibly taken or stolen much industry from Eastern Europe and bought and stolen much from other nations, especially the United States. But it also has produced creatively. It excels the rest of the world in some areas of technical inventions and scientific development.

This is not meant to give approval to the Communist system. The people behind the Iron Curtain have little freedom of expression and many of the people under Russian Communism would like to be rid of Communist control. This dictatorial police control is dehumanizing and too restricting to individual human development. Its stability is based on nationalism and the might of secret police and not on moral absolutes. It has produced more social responsibility than we now see in the United States, but fear and hypocrisy prevail because of government domination.

The motivational power of Russian Communism is the type which will be short-lived. There are two kinds of motivation: intrinsic and extrinsic. An extrinsic motivation is one that compels to action by external pressure, such as when you put a pistol to one's head and say,

"Do it." Obedience will cease once the pistol is removed. Intrinsic motivation comes from internal volition. One desires to do something from the heart out of love or because it is right. Russia's family is maintained by extrinsic motivation for Communism. If Russia rises to its goal of world power or allows consumer greed to become dominant, it may soon lose the ability to motivate and maintain its control. If so, the system will disintegrate rapidly. America began with an intrinsic motivation. Faith in God and obedience to His revealed commands because of His love was what formed the ethical standard taught in the family until recent years. This desperately needs to be restored.

Is Russia Really a Threat?

The Soviet Union is a rapidly rising threat to all the West in general and to the United States in particular. What happens to Europe is vital to the United States. Senator Sam Nunn of the Senate Armed Services Committee has said, "The NATO countries comprise the largest concentration of industrial capacity in the world, a population larger than that of either the United States or the Soviet Union, and an aggregate gross national product greater than that of the United States and twice as big as Russia."

He pointed out the vulnerability of NATO countries to Soviet power: "One fact is inarguable: The current condition of NATO's conventional defenses—poorly deployed troops, shortages of communication and equipment, cumbersome command and control—puts the alliance's effectiveness as a deterrent to aggression in serious question."[6]

Russia has worked out detailed ways to assemble a surprise strike force without detection by intelligence of the West. It also has already amassed huge forces on the border of West Germany.

In spite of its lack of conventional preparedness, NATO adopted a policy that it will use nuclear weapons only if the Soviets use nuclear weapons first or if NATO forces are threatened with destruction. It has in effect already told Russia it will fight with its nuclear hand tied behind its back.

Through detente and the Strategic Arms Limitation Treaty (SALT), Russia has taken advantage of the West. Brezhnev told the Eastern European Communist party leaders in 1973, "By 1985 as a consequence of what we are now achieving with detente, we will have achieved most of our objectives in Western Europe. . . . Come 1985, *we will be able to extend our will wherever we need to*" (italics mine). The signing of the SALT II agreement in June, 1979, if adopted by the Senate, could extend that advantage. Lt. General Edward Rowny, who served in SALT talks under three presidents, resigned after the SALT II signing because he felt it gave Russia too great a strategic armament advantage. General Alexander Haig, former Commander of NATO, and Lt. General Daniel O. Graham, former head of defense intelligence, also oppose it.

It has been said by Nunn and others that if Soviet forces invade Europe NATO might not last a month. If present trends continue, in a few years the NATO nations will be so overpowered that they may capitulate and go along with the Russians and do whatever they say, as Brezhnev said.

In the past decade the Soviets have risen from a position of marked military inferiority to the United States to one of clear military advantage. Lt. Gen. Graham said, "By most standards of measuring military forces, the Soviets have surpassed or are surpassing us. . . ." This viewpoint has been expressed by Senator Sam Nunn, former Secretary of Defense Melvin Laird, and General Haig of NATO. The gap between U. S. and Russian strength is widening every year. The following 1978 chart released by the Department of Defense shows the contrast:

THE MILITARY BALANCE: RUSSIA vs. U.S.

STRATEGIC WEAPONS

Intercontinental Ballistic Missiles

U.S.S.R.	1,477
U.S.	1,054

Submarine-Launched Ballistic Missiles

U.S.S.R.	909
U.S.	656

Long-Range Bombers

U.S.S.R.	195
U.S.	373

Warheads
Long-range missiles and bombers can deliver this many nuclear warheads—

U.S.S.R.	3,826
U.S.	11,330

CONVENTIONAL FORCES

Naval Ships

U.S.S.R.	1,092
U.S.	468

Combat Aircraft (other than long-range bombers)

U.S.S.R.	4,475
U.S.	7,585

Tanks

U.S.S.R.	45,000
U.S.	10,000

Helicopters

U.S.S.R.	3,800
U.S.	9,000

Artillery Weapons

U.S.S.R.	19,000
U.S.	5,000

MANPOWER
Active-Duty Force

U.S.S.R.	4.4 MILLION
U.S.	2.1 MILLION

There are significant factors not obvious in this chart released by the Defense Department. The Soviets have several areas of superiority. Their new SS18 Intercontinental Ballistic Missile can carry 45 MIRV warheads the size of our Poseidon missile. Their new missile for their submarines, the SSNB, has a range of 5,750 miles, compared to our Trident I with 4,000 miles. They also have developed a mobile launch for ICBM's. It is now known that the Soviets are nearing a breakthrough in developing a "gigaton" hydrogen bomb, which is equal to one billion tons of TNT, or 100 times more powerful than the largest current bomb (Hiroshima's bomb was equivalent to 15,000 tons of TNT). They are also developing knockout satellites and a fleet of super aircraft carriers. The U. S. B52 long-range bombers are very old and not equivalent to the newer long-range Russian bombers. Russian ground troops are transported in new amphibious BMP-60 mechanized combat vehicles which the troops can fire from inside, while NATO troops have traditional personnel carriers requiring unloading for firing. Moreover, their hand guns and artillery are superior to those of America, according to some unbiased authorities.

The Russians are dead serious about the use of chemical warfare. They have over 200,000 tons of nerve gas, and one-third of their troops are trained and equipped to use it. They have tanks and carrier vehicles that have sealed doors and gun ports and protective suits and inflatable sealed shelters. It is estimated the use of this would have an 80% casualty rate. It could be dropped on cities or used on the field of battle, destroying people, but not property, and could linger three or four days, killing almost instantly. The U.S. has one-fifth the nerve gas of Russia and little equipment and training to use it. Two billion dollars has been allotted to catch up in this.

The Soviets are spending 12 to 15% of their gross national product for military armament, compared to 5.5% of the gross national product of the United States. They produce 75% for the military and only 25% for civilian consumption, while the reverse is true for the United States. A major reason U. S. military spending has been curtailed is because it is the easiest way for

Congress to curb inflation without angering the voters. Defense spending has been cut almost in half from 1969 (43.5% of the budget) to 1976 (24.8%). Some congressmen are currently seeking to change this trend, but if inflation continues this may worsen.

Graphs released by the Defense Department in 1978 as presented on pages 196 and 197 show how America has been consistently falling behind Russia.

At the same time America's B52's are wearing out, President Carter is holding up the new B1 bomber. He also delayed production of the neutron bomb—the weapon the Russians fear most. Moreover, the Soviets currently spend one billion dollars on civil defense, training more than twenty million people in civil defense annually. They have prepared to evacuate their major cities to rural areas, underground, and aboard ships. They estimate they would lose "only ten million lives" in a nuclear exchange. The Communists killed about six million of their own people in forcing the communization of agriculture, and might feel such a price is worth gaining world domination.[7] The United States has no effective plan for civil defense, and a current estimate made for the U. S. government says there could be a loss of 165 million American lives in a nuclear attack.[8]

Pentagon military planners consider a combination of developments in the Soviet Union—"the massive build-up of strategic nuclear strength, and expansion of the civil defense system are evidence that the Kremlin has embraced a doctrine aimed not only at deterring nuclear war *but fighting one*" (italics mine).[9]

If the Soviets should gain control of Europe, the United States would be in an almost impossible situation even if we were not directly attacked. But most Americans do not realize that Russia is already in a threatening position to the United States. Senator Sam Nunn has also said, "Over the past 15 years, the Soviet Union has

CHANGES IN U.S./U.S.S.R. STRATEGIC WEAPONS

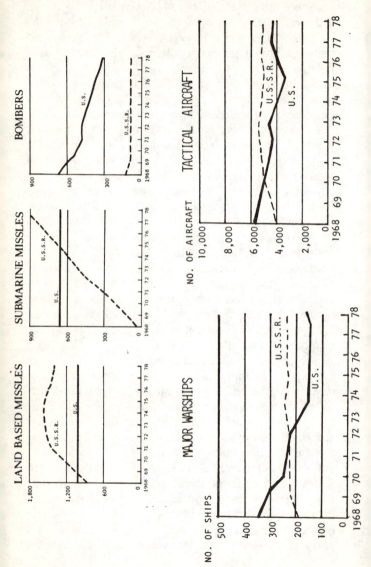

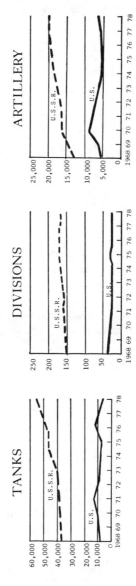

U.S./U.S.S.R. GROUND FORCE TRENDS(1968-1978)

expanded its military capability, both qualitatively and quantitatively. It has transformed itself from a regional into a global military power *which could be used directly against the citizens of our country*" (italics mine).[10]

There is a direct threat in the following ways:

Cuba has so-called defensive missiles that can reach many U. S. cities. Cuba now has submarines furnished by Russia, and perhaps mobile missile launchers also. In November, 1978, Russia gave Cuba twenty MiG 23 aircraft which are known to have nuclear capabilities. The Russians already have an entire brigade of Russian soldiers stationed in Cuba and are gradually increasing this number. In addition, there are over 6,000 Russian military advisors.

Russian aircraft fly within 200 miles of the east coast of the United States regularly. In only a matter of minutes they could turn those flights inland toward American cities.

Russian submarines with nuclear capabilities to destroy all American cities cruise off American shores regularly. The Russians have a new Alfa-class attack submarine designed to find and destroy our nuclear submarines, and which is superior to anything we have like it.

Russian ICBM's can be launched from fixed silos in Russia. They also have mobile platforms from which to launch nuclear warheads. Lt. General Daniel O. Graham has warned that even with the SALT II agreement the Russians can covertly produce the SS16 missile and launch these from mobile platforms. There is no way all of these can be knocked out.

Russian "suitcase nuclear bombs", to be detonated by radio impulse, are a threat to U. S. cities. Smugglers have brought thousands of tons of drugs into America by boat and aircraft, and "suitcase nuclear bombs" could be brought in with equal ease. The iron curtain deters the United States or any enemy from doing this to the Soviets.

The Soviet Union is already a formidable sword that is being raised to strike. America can no longer deny this as a real possibility. Unless the people of the United States turn back to God, renew their spiritual roots, and revive the family, God will certainly send judgment upon the nation. Every other nation that has followed the course of decay now occurring in America has been destroyed. While we should be prepared militarily, our fear should be of God and not of Russia (Proverbs 21:31; Psalm 33:13–22; 44:6–8; 60:11,12). God can stay the sword if America is repentant.

However, the Bible teaches that before God sends the sword of destruction He uses the rod of correction. The rod of correction is often economic scarcity. In the Bible God sent famine, plagues of insects (See "The Great Insect Invasion," *U. S. News and World Report,* February 19, 1979), military spoiling and destruction, earthquakes and the like. These warnings were intended to lead the people to repent (Isaiah 1:5–8; Jeremiah 4:10–13; 5:11–18; Hosea 4:1–5; Joel 1:1–15; Amos 4:6–13; 1 Kings 17:1ff). Even Sodom and Gomorrah were warned by being invaded and spoiled by the four kings allied under Chedorlaomer (Genesis 14:1–12). On the basis of this biblical principle, God may warn America through a great economic crisis and/or great earthquakes. It may be that the economic crisis beginning in 1979 is God's last warning. If we do not repent, God's judgment of the Russian sword may come.

America may be near to feeling the rod of correction. William E. Simon, in his book *A Time for Truth,* has shown that there is no inherent reason for America to have an economic crisis, but that the interventionist bureaucratic philosophy, the greed of American businessmen, and the greed of the people are driving her in that direction. Government control of energy resources and strangulation of business have curtailed productivity and drained off the supply of capital.

While America is the world's bread basket now, scarcity of food could occur. The American independent farmer has been caught in the squeeze of greed which is causing the rise of the price of farm equipment, fertilizer, seed and other supplies on one side, and the rise of transportation costs and wholesale prices on the other, so that agricultural production is threatened by government restraint on food prices to hold down inflation. American farm debt has doubled since 1970, and farm income, adjusted for inflation, is down to about what it was in 1940. Independent farmers are rapidly selling out to big corporations. America's large food and energy resources are ironically being restrained just when they are significantly needed. While the United States is still the world's largest food producer, problems are growing.

I believe only a genuine spiritual and moral renewal can prevent the coming needless crisis.

When Might a U. S. Crisis Come?

While the Russians have Siberian oil deposits (48 billion barrels), these are difficult to get to, and they will likely be in a crucial oil shortage by 1985. If they reach military dominance by 1985 as they plan, they will be in a geographical position to force the sale of Middle Eastern oil only to them, thereby bringing an economic/energy crisis on the U. S. Their interference in Iran, their military takeover of Afghanistan, and their intervention in Africa are aimed at putting them in a position of military power to shut off oil to the West and to gain strategic materials from Africa. The Russians are also nearing the end of world credit, and in a few years may not be able to borrow on the world market.

Hence, present trends point to a crisis for the United States about 1985. I do not present this as a definite date, but as a reasonable estimate. Even though things do not usually proceed as rapidly as expected, spiritual renewal that will change the family and renew social stability is urgent. The people of the United States need to humble themselves, pray for God's blessing and begin immediately to promote a turning back to God and His will in responsible human relationships. This is needed now!

It is biblical to be prepared militarily but not to put faith in this alone. America's best course for defense is to trust the living God and not weapons such as missiles, tanks, planes, guns or ships or alliances. If we put our trust in Him He will restrain all enemies and He will enable us to have whatever defenses are needed. God, speaking through the psalmist, said, "I want you to trust Me in your times of trouble, so I can rescue you, and you can give Me glory" (Psalm 50:15, Living Bible).

Part Three

POSITIVE STEPS
FOR RENEWAL

Chapter 14

DETERMINING A COURSE OF ACTION TO RENEW THE FAMILY

Return from Individualism to Social Responsibility

It has been shown that in the decay of many nations the last stages move from the emphasis on the good of society and community to that of the individual, finally destroying the family and social relationships. In the years when America had God-centered homes, men and women were seen to be valuable as individuals in the sight of God and were responsible to love God and *neighbor* as self. Those *nearest* to the man were his wife and children. As decay progressed, the individual man saw himself more and more as important within himself and minimized his responsibilities to God and his wife and children. This led to selfish individualism by women also, and in turn to selfish individualism by youth. The emphasis focused more on one's rights and on the responsibility of the state to provide for *him or her* and defend his or her rights. Thus, political collectivism (socialism) replaced individual responsibility.[1]

Meaningful social action, therefore, should aim at renewal of a responsible relationship to God and the family. A renewal of a public consciousness of God should be accompanied by a renewal of sex roles within the family.

A renewal of men's relationship to God and their spiritual leadership of the family is the supreme need. That need will be focused on in the last chapter. If there is renewed commitment to God in the family, the family will again become the school to learn how to care for others. We should move away from the idea of the rights and privileges of the individual alone, but in so doing we should not deny the *value* of the individual before God. Such an effort against individualism will go against the grain of all modern thought and will cause shock and reaction. We should be prepared to proclaim truth lovingly in that direction and *persist* on its rightness regardless of the reaction. That is the only conceivable way the public mindset can be shifted back toward social responsibility. While some of the suggestions given in the following pages may go against the grain of your thinking at first, please think them through as a means for strengthening the family.

Four Institutions to Influence

To effect renewal, there are four institutions through which efforts of change should be carried out. They are the family, the church, the business community (including the mass media), and the government (including public education). It has been argued that the family is the foundation for all the others and the main point of sickness today (Chapter Two). Therefore the family must first be changed from within, but if the laws and customs of the other institutions are not modified to allow for those changes, they will have difficulty working. For example, if a father wants to spend time in the evenings with his family, but the church requires participation two or three nights a week, he will do it with great difficulty. If mothers and fathers in a school district decide to teach their own sex education with a God-centered emphasis at home, but the school board will not delete its course, the children could be very confused. Hence, commitment within the family must lead to determined efforts outside it.

Make the Family Priority

The first and most important step of renewal of the home is for men and women to change personally their thought and *practice* about family. The man especially must make this his emphasis. He needs to spend time with his wife and children and see that the children are his responsibility as well as his wife's. This needs to become a daily thing, and not just when he plans a two-week vacation once a year. The man needs to be the leader in fun and games, in work together, and in training in the things of God. His spiritual leadership should not just center around a time of Bible reading and prayer, though that is needed, but around discussing all aspects of life from a God-centered perspective. The man needs to set the example of thinking things from God's point of view, of trusting God for material things, of discussing sex as sacred and God-given, to be used as He designed it, and in relating all issues of life to the Lord. He should show his family that it is appropriate to pray about any and all things.

Men and women need to begin to understand and appreciate their differences as from the Lord. Women need to appreciate the man's need to be involved part of the time in meaningful creative work with other men. God made man this way, and it is for the benefit of his wife and children so he can adequately provide. But men need to appreciate the fact that women also need to contribute to intellectual and creative efforts with them and with other women in the community. Men need to recognize the fact that their wives desire the appreciation and respect of their husbands more than anyone, and men should therefore take great care in how they give directions. Leadership can best be by *helping* to do something differently and by questions that would suggest a different way of doing things, rather than by saying, "You are wrong." Criticism can be wounding, and repeated criticism can crush a spirit and kill love.

The man should regularly and at special times communicate with his wife to plan and carry out their family life. He should ask for her advice and help in everything. He should learn to trust Christ to change his wife and children when they don't perform as he thinks they should, and the wife should prayerfully trust Christ to change her husband (1 Peter 3:1–9). Religion can be an intolerable burden in a home where the husband is constantly on his wife to be what he legalistically thinks she should be, and she is constantly nagging and badgering him to be what she thinks he should be. More praise and prayer with trust in Christ to correct and direct the home is essential to the man's leadership and the wife's response. The Lord Jesus Christ is alive and is perfectly able to correct a disobedient wife or husband (Romans 14:4,9,10; Hebrews 12:5–11).

When men and women both begin to show they trust God in their home life, this will do more to restore the unity of the family and transform our nation from individual thinking than anything else. Training men to lead their homes is a church responsibility that will be discussed later. But all the church and political activity to renew sex roles and social relationships will be useless without individual commitment to this. When the men of America begin to take the lead in this, then appropriate business, church, or political action will be meaningful.

Encourage Business Leaders to Renew the Family

In Chapter Six we pointed out the serious problems, economic and otherwise, that the business community is facing. The greed, decline of the family, and consequent moral breakdown in society are the main causes of these problems. The increasing control of government bureaucracy imposes greater costs in reporting and operating to meet government standards. The growing tax burden is taking its toll on profits. Theft and dishonesty by workers and customers is also a burden that is in part a by-product of the moral breakdown of the family. The strong individualism of workers expressed in an independence from management, complaints and demands about their jobs, and high absenteeism are growing problems and add to reduced productivity.

Business and labor need to be shown that a renewal of the family is to their advantage—indeed, an urgent need for them. Information can be disseminated through articles in business and union magazines, and literature could be circulated at business and union meetings. The churches can make known the importance of family renewal for the working community at their meetings. Business and union leaders themselves can sponsor speakers who will talk on this subject. Management might invite speakers to address their workers in their parking lots at shift changes or at meetings held on company time.

In the next chapter there are suggestions that business and industry can begin to do to help the family. Business and union leaders could do research themselves as to what can be done to help renew the family in America. Leaders can themselves begin to set an example of giving priority to their families and encourage other leaders to do the same.

Two Agencies of Authority—Church and State

Jesus indicated that there were two God-given organizations of authority to which men must give allegiance: the state and the church. "Render to Caesar the things that are Caesar's, and to God the things that are God's" (Matthew 22:21; Mark 12:17; Luke 20:25). He reminded the pagan Pilate, Caesar's representative, that his power was God-given (John 19:11). Paul saw the church as the body of Christ, proclaiming Christ to the world. As such, the church was to use rational persuasion and suffering love (II Timothy 2:23–26; Romans 12:17–21; cf. Matthew 5:41–48). But Paul saw the civil governing authority as a minister of God, bearing the sword. It is the one that avenges against anyone who does moral wrong, and therefore is the protector of Christians (Romans 13:1–7). The power of the church is in the persuading of the conscience, while the power of human government is in physical force. The church seeks to persuade men to submit voluntarily to the authority of God in Christ and come under the regular teaching, guidance, and oversight of the church. The state is over all men within its borders and requires obedience to its laws, whether they wish to submit or not.

The church includes men from all national states, and to try to identify it with any one state denies the transnational authority of Christ. While Christ will unite church and state at His final glorious return in power, we go contrary to the word of Christ to try to make any one state a tool of the church in this age. This was a mistake of the church in the Middle Ages and in the early Puritan governmental ideal.[2] The distinction of church and state is a unique New Testament concept. In the Old Testament there was a theocracy of the church and one nation, Israel. In the New Testament the church includes the world and cannot be linked with any one nation.

Believers have already accepted the benefits of Christ's love and in response have submitted to Him. It is their calling through the church to win men to God's eternal kingdom and to proclaim and exemplify the moral ideals of God's Word. On the other hand, the state should uphold the laws of God required by Christ's work of creation and the benefits *all men* enjoy in nature. It is right to expect the leaders of the state to be committed to a general theism as a national civil religion. Violation of the laws of God in nature threatens the continuation of society, while upholding them preserves the life and health of the majority of the people. The Ten Commandments are applicable to all men and are written in man's conscience (Romans 2:13–15). The maintaining of the family is important for all men and is based on God's working in the laws of nature. Human government should pass and maintain laws to uphold the family. But the state should not be used to force people to accept Christ and become a part of the church, even though the ideal of the family is accomplished best under submission to Christ. God's kingdom is built by *voluntary submission* to Christ the King. The genius of the success of the Christian family is based on that voluntary submission to Christ in the family roles.

The church and the state in America are both very complex in the way they operate. To examine these, and the forces that influence them, would take a diversion from the main thesis of this book. But it is important to understand the way we should seek to influence both. The church must proclaim to the world the ideals of Christ, but those in the church have no right to force submission to Christ's ideals through the state. The American forefathers were correct in seeing the need of the

separation of church and state. The uniting of the church
and state under Constantine (313 AD) led to intense persecution and religious wars until the Edict of Toleration
in 1687 and the Peace of Westphalia in 1643. This point
is stressed because the pressures are growing to obliterate
the distinctions of church and state.

Forces to Remove Church and State Distinction

As the family diminishes and individualism grows, cult
groups take advantage of the insecurity of people and
their intense desire to relate meaningfully to another person or group. The leaders of those groups then exploit
the people for money, political power, and often sex. This
trend has skyrocketed in the United States in recent years
and is demonstrated in the phenomenal growth of the
Children of God, the movement of Sun Myung Moon,
the events connected with Jim Jones and the People's
Temple, the controversy in the Worldwide Church of
God of Herbert W. Armstrong, and many others. Government is finding that it has reasons to intervene in these
matters to protect people from wolves in sheep's clothing.

Also, liberal educators and politicians are seeking to
interfere with the growing number of Christian day
schools because in some there has been racial discrimina-
tion and because these liberal educators wish to control
and regulate standards of academic requirements. Hence,
the distinction between church and state is being blurred
and could lead to state control of the church, with the
complete exaltation of secular humanism in the years
ahead. This will be antichristian, and against the very
protection America's founders intended to insure by separating church and state.

Another group who is seeking to remove the distinction
of church and state is ecclesiastical leaders who want
political power. Generally speaking, these are clergymen

who may profess faith in Christ as taught in the New Testament but who in fact feel *they* must force people to change rather than bring them to know Christ and let His Spirit change their lives. Their faith is not as much in the power of the word of God, proclaimed and taught, as in their ability to legislate for others. These may be conservative or liberal in their thinking; Jesus warned of the Pharisees (conservatives) and Sadducees (liberals). They may be leaders in Protestant, Roman Catholic, or other groups, and there may be those who truly believe in Christ among them.[3]

Christians in Politics

While under the Roman imperial government the early Christians had no way for influencing change but to pray for kings (1 Timothy 2:2), in America we have the privilege by our votes to influence the government to pass laws. But instead of getting the churches involved in a political mission, the church can influence its members to establish and support a political lobby group or groups outside its control to achieve its ends through the major parties. There are now such lobby groups as the Christian Voice, directed by Robert G. Grant, with headquarters in Pasadena, California, Jerry Falwell's Moral Majority, and many others. These should *not* aim at establishing a Christian state as some of these do, but government based on God's laws in nature. To this, individual Christians, not the churches, should contribute their money, prayers and efforts to pass laws to renew and safeguard the family. Such change needs to be promoted directly in business, education, industry, and labor unions *which affect the governmental process.* If this political effort is broadly theistic (not uniquely Christian) then all men will feel free to support its efforts. Great effort must be made to allow free expression of all views of people who believe in God so that the lobbying groups are not the narrow views of a few men.

The church itself should continue to proclaim Christ and call its members to a public declaration of the ideals of the Christian family and lifestyle, while discipling its people to *live* what it proclaims. It should aim at converting all men to the kingdom of God by love and reason. The worst thing the church could do is to forsake its spiritual mission for politics.

There will be increasing efforts in the years ahead to get Christians involved in political rallies. This is good, but if Christians do this and do not also have a public declaration of Christian ideals, the national civil religion will not be renewed. We will end up wearing ourselves out in running to one political fire after the other, with only temporary results. The public witness of the united church is much more important.

The next chapter aims at suggesting general objectives for renewing the family through government and public institutions. Chapter Sixteen, which follows that, is a description of a way in which I believe Christians can corporately proclaim Christ and Christian family ideals and move toward training the Christian father and mother to be mature and know how to establish a genuinely Christian family. This latter is the most important step for dynamic renewal. The public proclamation of ideals by the church will help renew the national civil religion.

Affect the Leadership

An effective community strategy will aim at influencing the actions of public decision makers. While everyone may contribute meaningfully, we cannot all contribute equally, as much as some may want to think so. Sober reflection will lead to the conclusion that in almost every large group there is a controlling group who make the decisions and plot the course of action. A. W. Tozer once said, "The public is never capable of acting in masse. Without a leader it is headless, and a headless body is powerless. Always someone must lead. Even the mob engaged in pillage and murder is not the disorganized thing it appears to be. Someone behind the violence is a leader whose ideas it is simply putting into effect."[4]

Fortunately, in America the vote still influences the governmental process, even though the democratic process is in grave danger. There is still opportunity for all men to unite together to change the direction the leaders go, if we have the commitment and the help of God. To influence leaders we must influence public opinion. We need to use the influence of the mass media and other means to help in accomplishing this.

The leaders today in most areas of society, even in much of the church, are committed to a secular humanistic point of view that promotes and defends the individual man over against society and the glory of God. If renewal of the family and our nation is to be attained, we must recognize this as a hard reality and accept the fact that change will come with great difficulty and suffering. We must be committed to achieve our goals, beginning now and continuing *no matter how long it takes.*

Moreover, we must recognize that initial changes may be made by trying to modify the actions of the present leadership. Our long-range goal should be to raise up new leaders, men and women, who understand the causes of decay in society and who are committed to a vital and active faith in God to guide the future. To modify the actions of the present leaders there will need to be strong public proclamation of the ideals of God in the family while we work toward practical implementation of renewed family relationships. We must be careful, however, not to be hypocritical—what we proclaim publicly we must be committed to in our lives. Our family relationships must reflect this commitment.

Chapter 15

SUGGESTED GENERAL OBJECTIVES FOR RENEWAL OF THE FAMILY

In introducing this chapter on general objectives for renewing the family, it needs to be again said that achieving such objectives is dependent on personal commitment to spiritual renewal in the family and a public witness of the church to biblical family ideals. Considerations for action in that most important area are reserved for the last chapter, as already mentioned.

Also, these general objectives must be carried out primarily in the public sector by the efforts of those who hold a general theistic view of life. The objective therefore is to influence the public mind and not primarily the church or the Christian individual. The effort is therefore to seek to get people to return to social responsibility for self-interest, rather than because of Christian love and devotion, although those motives are the most valid ones.

The suggestions in this chapter are meant to stimulate thought and not to serve as final answers. Much careful and prayerful evaluation is needed on these issues before action is taken, and it will take some time before such things can be achieved.

How to Help Children

As the unity and strength of the family disintegrates into self-centered individualism, the children are hurt in many ways and lack security and real purpose. We need to do everything we possibly can to prevent and alleviate these hurts.

One example of harm to children is physical abuse. We must educate people through the mass media and the churches to understand that child abuse is often a product of competition and hate between father and mother, or hostilities transmitted from the parents of parents. These are usually produced because the parents' primary objectives are attainment of material wealth, social status, and personal selfish pleasure. While children must be protected from parental abuse, the change of attitudes and relationships of fathers and mothers toward each other and toward their children is the primary need. Parents must be shown that children can bring happiness and be valuable to them—that the long-term satisfaction of having raised well-adjusted children is greater than any other benefit of life. Well-developed children are an asset to society. Abortion, neglect, and abuse of children are the most tragic aspects of family decay.

There is a great need to change our philosophy of child training from one that exalts the individual and teaches him to be primarily independent and self-centered to one that is theistic. The theistic view will acknowledge the uniqueness of each individual and his God-given talents, but also stress the fact that he was born of human parents into a world of other humans whom God created and to whom he has a responsibility. John Dewey's philosophy of public education was greatly influenced by post-Hegelian individualism. His philosophy and others such as existentialism, which also logically follow, have promoted the selfish individualism that is fragmenting our society, even though each had some valuable insights.

In training children, their involvement with their parents is very important. Under the modern educational philosophy they have become more separated from their parents and of less personal benefit to them. All children need to be taught they are responsible for helping their parents, even as the parents are responsible for supporting and protecting them. Many can be encouraged to help right in the vocation of their parents. They usually will have more understanding and appreciation of their parents as they learn more about their vocation. By more actively helping their parents, young people will develop more meaningful relationships and a sense of value and self-respect, and could be more willing to support their parents later on, when they are older or in need. Involvement of children in the work of their parents could be a motivation for some people to have children and care for them, and in the long run will relieve the state of many responsibilities for the care of older people.

As children work with their parents, many will become interested and want to enter the same work with them. Inherited traits and gifts and home-learned skills can often enable a child to succeed better in the same area of vocation as the parents, and this contributes much to social progress. Many people have done this. Further encouragement of young people along this line would help solve the frustrating search for vocation that many go through when they have the concept that every person should find his or her own unique vocation. There is nothing demeaning about being about our father's business (Luke 2:49; John 9:4, et al.). Also, children who work with their parents will feel like they are growing up and will not need to turn to drugs to try to feel big. However, some children *are* fitted for a unique vocation. Such an approach should not allow us to ignore the fact that some children will be uniquely called by God to special tasks and should be guided and encouraged by their parents to go in this direction.

In regard to children working with their parents, it might be helpful to encourage industry and business to evaluate ways in which youth could be paid to work with their parents as assistants. Perhaps laws allowing family apprenticeship with below-minimum-wage pay for beginners could be adopted to encourage such employment.

We need to give public recognition and rewards to youth who make significant contributions and achievements with their parents, and parents should be publicly commended for raising children who are an asset to the community.

We need to develop a biblical philosophy of discipline that goes beyond "spare the rod and spoil the child." Personal encouragement and rebuke are also scriptural, as well as public praise for achievements and development of talents. Withdrawal of privileges or exclusion from parents for misbehavior, as well as public rebuke in some cases, also have a place (John 14:21,32; Matthew 18:15–17; 1 Timothy 5:20). The more these things are consistently done in the home, the more they would be practiced in the church and community. Older youth can be involved in helping discipline too. As younger children look up to them, they can motivate them to work and to desire adult standards of behavior.

Our children need the educational policies that will enable them to develop normally in the best way. One thing to consider is that even though boys and girls are equal in value and intelligence, they *are* different and they develop at different rates and levels, young boys generally being a little behind girls of the same age. It could be best for both if part of their school time was coeducational and part separated. Many of the countries of the world have complete separation of the sexes in elementary and secondary education. In the Western nations coeducation prevails, and it is interesting that we are the ones experiencing the worst moral breakdown.

In promoting this policy, considerable study is needed to determine what courses would be best coeducational and which separate. There should be separate training at least in marriage responsibilities, physical education, and competitive team sports. Many of the courses now taught together perhaps could continue that way, but if the different developmental levels of boys and girls could be taken into account by testing and grading them separately, it could relieve the discouragement many boys have in classroom situations, and could remove sex competition. At colleges, mixed dorms and common baths obviously do not respect sexual differences and should be excluded.

Today many young men and women are assuming many of the responsibilities of adulthood at the age of eighteen, often to regret it later. It would be to their advantage, as well as helpful to society, if they remain under the authority of their parents until the age of twenty. This was the age of adult accountability in the nation of Israel (Exodus 30:14; Numbers 14:29, et al.). The Bible indicates that the young woman should have the right to decide on her marriage partner, but the final authority should rest with her father (1 Corinthians 7:36–38; Genesis 24:51–58, et al.). This view is mid-way between the Eastern practice of marriages arranged by parents and the current Western practice of young people living with or marrying whom they desire without parental counsel. This position also considers the value of society as well as that of the individual.

How to Help Women

Across America more and more women have a negative attitude toward the priority of motherhood. There are many reasons for this, such as individualism, self-centeredness, the conditioning of prevailing social attitudes, fear of responsibility, or fear of population growth. Therefore many women, even many mothers, are missing the balance and fulfillment that their unique physiology and psychology should be giving them. There are many things that can help to get this balance back.

We should honor and reward women who have children and raise them, and do it with sincerity and real respect. Having children and raising them for the glory of God and the good of society is vital. In men's battle in the marketplace, they have taken this for granted.

We should emphasize that while women have a distinct biology, that biology is tied to a whole person with mental and creative abilities. Women should not be asked to go back to being only mothers and housewives, as was suggested by the psychological movement in the middle of the century (cf. pp. 58–60), without giving the operation of the home real value. We need to do whatever we can, both in attitudes and practices, to give this role for women its full meaning. Otherwise we will not slow down the deterioration of society.

Women need to be made aware of the fact that, while there is still a worldwide population threat, that threat has diminished somewhat. In 1977 the world population growth was the lowest in recorded history, dropping from 30 per thousand in 1976 to 29. In America the birth rate is very near the death rate. The explosive birth rate is in the more undeveloped nations. The production of most food and goods can best be done by educated and advanced nations like America, and the world could benefit by an increase of our birth rate. More than two children per family are needed just to replenish the population. Moreover, nations with an older population that is not being renewed lose their desire and power to defend them-

selves. Future American defense is threatened by our declining birth rate.

We need to refute forcefully the trends of modern thinking by restoring an emphasis on the good of sex for procreation, doing this in such a way that sex for pleasure
is given its right meaning and balance as to importance.
This is very important for the long-term self-interest and
fulfillment of a woman, and is very important for men
also. Sex rightly is a pleasure the man desires to bestow
on his wife because he cares for her and wants to make
her happy as his full partner and the future mother of
their children. It is a pleasure the wife offers to her husband because she cares for him, respects him, and appreciates him as her partner, the one who fathers her children,
the one who will provide and protect her when she bears
and nurses them, and the one who is willing to help her
reach her broadest fulfillment as a person. When sex is
sought primarily for selfish pleasure, it diminishes the
personal relationship instead of enhancing it.

The sex act finds its greatest satisfaction as a man and
woman who love each other join their physical and spiritual beings in their offspring. There can be great mutual
joy in having children, raising them together, and developing their minds, their creative skills, and their moral
characters so they can honor God and help carry on
and build a better world for tomorrow. When a man
and woman miss this and end up competing for more
money, for success, and then for the affection of their
children, they have sold their blessings for a mess of pot-
tage.

It would be helpful to women to have encouragement
for their integral involvement with their children at
school. One way would be to elect a female board of
guidance on school activities that can be a real adjunct
to what is usually a male school board that deals with

dollars, courses and credentials. Another way is to use mothers and older children to help teach, under skilled and qualified direction.

Many things can be researched and developed to give women more opportunities for realistic creative work beyond their normal involvement in the home. The following are a few suggestions.

Cooperatively owned child-care centers could be formed for mothers of the same community, which would allow mothers personal experiences with their own children while allowing time for developing skills and producing marketable products. The growing number of older women in the population could also be given meaningful employment by helping part-time in this.

New forms of home industry which can employ husband, wife, and children could be developed. It is feasible that our modern technology, using small computers and machines, could today develop home industry that would be financially profitable, while this might not have been possible fifteen years ago. Big business or government might provide the capital, and a retail business could market the product of a number of homes. The wife and children would receive a new sense of value, and the family would be meaningfully productive again. Large business corporations need to think more in terms of family units than just individuals. This would be, in the long run, more advantageous for them as well. Business corporations in other countries, such as Japan, have been successfully family oriented.

Government and business can be encouraged to plan ways for women to develop so they can move into the public sector and contribute their abilities in a full-time way after their children are grown. Government help should be by tax incentives for the schooling and training, and not by subsidy or federal programs. Safeguards need to be implemented to prevent sexual temptations from intimate working relationships between men and women on the same job.

We need to urge change in Social Security and inheritance laws so women whose husbands divorce them and remarry will receive a proportion of their husband's financial accumulation according to the years of marriage. This will help protect women against and in divorce, and will encourage them to help their husbands.

We can encourage and help unmarried women to be trained and find jobs that will bring maximum fulfillment in the use of their talents. Their full meaningful employment is best for them and the community also. The church especially needs to furnish a good social atmosphere for single women and men, out of concern for them and to give them opportunity for the best kinds of marriages. Today the downtown areas of our large cities are being occupied by large numbers of young single people, many of whom find their social life mainly in singles bars and swinging parties.

It is important to have fairness both to women and their employers. Business and industry should be encouraged to employ women in appropriate jobs, and they are more capable at some than are men. They should be required to give women and men equal pay for equal work and equal expense. There can be an increased cost in employing women, however, since many of them must be away from their jobs more often than men because of female problems, pregnancies, and family needs. Often substitutes and retraining costs are involved. These additional costs need to be evaluated, and women should be willing to help compensate their employer for those so that he will not be penalized in the market competition because he has hired women. This could make it easier for women to find jobs since a major objection to their employment would be removed.

When wives are working outside the home, it is important that they and their husbands cooperate in the disposition of their finances. It would be good for a wife to join her earnings with those of her husband in a joint bank account and together decide the use of the joint funds, at the same time having certain funds available for each to use freely for personal use.

How to Help Men and Parents in General

The main burden for leading and providing for the family lies with the husband and father. This is a long, hard, and very responsible task, and men need every encouragement to accomplish it well. Unfortunately, many trends of modern thinking do not help to give men confidence in this role. We need to do all we can to refute these trends.

We need to restore the sexual identity of the man and husband. When a woman lets a man penetrate her and a child is conceived, it belongs as much to him as it does to her, if he is willing to make the long-range commitment in marriage to help care for her and the child. It is wrong to say that a woman's body is her own and she has the sole right to abort the child. The facts demand that the man be given personal and legal power along with the woman. The fetus would never exist without her consent to him and his contribution of the sperm that started its growth. She made a moral commitment to him when she conceived.

While the Right to Life movement may speak rightfully for the unborn child, legal restrictions will never solve the abortion problem. There will be an ever-increasing number of women conceiving unwanted children unless love and sacrificially caring responsibility are restored to sex. A correction of the roles and relationships of the sexes is the main way to control abortion and all the other growing evils of hate-ridden and fragmented homes.

We need also to distinguish areas of work and recreation as being masculine. The executive leadership and decision-making roles in business and politics would best be maintained for men, but women would be needed in top advisory jobs that require equal intellectual competence. The reason for this is that most women cannot easily participate in intense argumentation over issues without emotional involvement, as can most men. Men can argue, decide, and go away and forget it, while an attack on a woman's point of view becomes a personal attack for most women.

Rough physical jobs requiring strength and involving danger—such as military fighting, much police work, and most construction work—should be reserved for men. Certain sports are obviously masculine, yet women are attempting to participate even in some of these. There is a need to establish these sports definitely as masculine, based on physiological and medical studies of the different qualities of men and women. The trend in the courts is to break down these distinctions, so legislation is needed to establish them—in every area in which they are needed.

Men and boys need to be educated to understand how important it is to communicate with women, and they need help in knowing how to communicate. They need to understand better how women are different and what some of the basic rules of communication are. In interviewing many young women and counseling with women in general, I have found that one of the most common failures of husbands and fathers is that of not communicating. The church, church schools, and public schools could offer training in this.

Women also need training about the differences of men. They especially need to understand that man's insistent sex drive and his desire for recognition can be greatly beneficial to a woman in motivating the man to care for her and their children. If women understand this, they will not react to these qualities in men and in love can use those traits for the benefit of the whole family.

We have already suggested that business and industry be encouraged to employ women in appropriate jobs and to give them equal pay with men for equal work. At the same time, there needs to be a balance in this. In recent years there has been a tendency by some to employ women over men simply to even the ratio or because of the demands of the women. This has put the economic situation of many families in jeopardy. In the long run this insecurity and weakening of the family will hurt these businesses as well. I suggest that where there is equal qualification for jobs, employers grant motherhood-preference to men whose wives have children. I mean by this that in cases in which a man is the only wage earner for a family with children, and a competing woman is the second wage earner for a family of smaller size, or a competing man has no family, the employer would give the job or the advancement to the father, if there is no significant difference in qualification. This would give full recognition to the importance of raising children and would help women to be secure and feel free to have children. This is being realistic about the strategic importance of the family and is saying to each woman that her husband has every chance for a job to care for his wife if she is willing to bear children and care for them. I am not advocating that this be made law (or be excluded by law), but that it be promoted as business policy, for the good of society and the best long-term interests of business as well.

We need to urge that laws be passed limiting restrictions against renting housing to families with children. If more and more housing excludes children, the decline in desire for children could snowball. However, there need to be safeguards for landlords, such as laws requiring parents to pay a fine for vandalism by their children, as well as paying for the damage.

When both parents of junior high and high school students work and their children are left unattended, there is a high rate of teen-age delinquency. There is a need for after-school community recreation by churches, apartment complexes, and local governments. If parents require their children to be involved and parents of the community help run these efforts, the children will be more open to adult standards. Also, research needs to be done as to what to do concerning the responsibility of parents when children are found delinquent or involved in crime. Perhaps the parents need to be fined, or if the delinquency is repeated, perhaps one parent should be made to quit work, and if it is repeated again the parent should perhaps be jailed also. These are drastic measures, but if something similar is not done, America will soon have teen-age groups that roam, pillage, and commit violent acts, as they have in other countries.

It would be helpful to families if employers, whether government or business, would grant time off to mothers and fathers during times when their children are out of school so they can be together. This parental preference over single employees concerning work hours and days off would allow parents more time to build a relationship with their children. Business and industry might even reorganize the work hours for parents with school children so they could go to work earlier and get home earlier to spend time with their children.

To help in renewing the extended family, many things could be done. For example, we could plan ways of linking homes for older people to nursery centers so that capable older women could help with their own grandchildren and other children, and so that working adults could come and be with both their parents and children at the same time.

One of the most important things we can do to help our families is to change and control the television so it can be used to serve us. An affordable video-tape or video-disc machine should soon be developed, and then parents can have more control of what is viewed. Programs can then be produced, recorded, and played to meet the spiritual, educational, and entertainment needs of the family. This will tear us away from the chains of the networks, which often cater to the flesh in order to make money. Moreover, it will allow us to control our time so that the television can be fitted into times when the family can be together. Even now churches and community groups could maintain video-tape or video-disc machines for rent or loan, and a library of tapes and discs suitable for the family.

Above all, men and women need to begin to think in terms of what they can do to serve their partner so they will become "one flesh." And society needs to think, act, and legislate in such a way as to promote unity of the family in marriage, and not just the rights of individuals.

Many ideas and suggestions have been given here. Some could be implemented into legislation, while others could best be carried out by school and church. But in passing legislation there should be great care not to establish government programs and bureaucracy that would control or interfere in our family life.

Chapter 16

THE PRIMARY SOLUTION—
MALE SPIRITUAL RENEWAL

Defining the Main Objective

To correct the decline of our nation a concerted effort should be made to attack the main source of the problem. The evidence presented in Parts One and Two shows that the root of the problem is men's spiritual failure. Instead of leading their families in the worship of God and caring about their wives and children as people, they have neglected these responsibilities in pursuit of wealth and worldly status. Men have worshiped mammon instead of God. We argued that other steps of decline automatically followed. *I am convinced, therefore, that correction of this main problem will automatically lead to change in all the other areas.*

The *most basic thing* I am saying is that renewal of the family and nation rests on *renewing the spiritual leadership of men.* While cooperation and assistance of women is needed, this will most readily take place after men's commitment to God occurs.

Therefore, the main need is to call men away from idolatrous pursuit of business and wealth and back to the worship of God and the priority of building the kingdom of God through the home, which is the germ cell of the church and society. This needs to include not only laymen in business and trades, but also men in the ministry. Many a man in Christian work has pursued a bigger church, larger salary, or higher attainment in his Christian organization and neglected his own family. Those in Christian ministry need to be the examples.

In calling men to forsake the pursuit of mammon over God, it needs to be made clear that this is not a call to loaf and lie around the house. One of the main responsibilities of the man is to be God's agent to provide for his family "by the sweat of his brow" and to care for his neighbor. At the same time, men should not "fix their hope on the uncertainty of riches, but on God, who richly supplies us with all things to enjoy" (1 Timothy 6:17,18).

There is a great need to restore respect for hard work and productive labor. Trust in money often leads to the desire for more pay for less work. In recent years the rate of productivity of Americans has dropped below that of many other nations of the world (see pp. 93, 94). The laws of God call for working six days as well as resting one. But work for the family need not cause neglect in spending time with them in worship, teaching, discipline and play. Too many men have excused their neglect of the family so they can have business success by saying, "I have to provide, don't I?"

Women of course need to be challenged to see the importance of being a wife, helper and mother. But until men turn their priority of values away from wealth and worldly attainment, women will find their roles difficult and unattractive. They will continue to pursue those perverted goals which men have established. The eager cooperation and encouragement of the wife will make it easier for the husband to trust God and put his wife and the family first for the Lord. Change by both men and women is needed. It may require a lower living standard as far as material things are concerned. But happiness comes more out of our relationship to God and others than out of what we possess.

Also, there is a need to challenge young single men and women to accept the biblical roles in the family and begin preparing now to fill those roles. This can be done by developing the right attitudes and habits that will make them good fathers and mothers. If young people would determine to marry only a person who is committed to the biblical roles, other young people would take these more seriously. Young people will be the ones to lose most in the future unless trends are changed.

How to Achieve the Objective?

Relate Evangelism to Family Renewal

How can a movement be started to turn men to God from mammon, to change the American family, and to promote national revival? Many have expected evangelistic and revivalistic preaching to cause great changes in society, as they did especially in the eighteenth and nineteenth centuries. Many evangelists have called for "revival in our time," but it has not come. While there is certainly a place for mass evangelism, perhaps this is not the main method for revival today. In fact, the emphasis on the individual's acceptance of Christ needs to be linked to the father's responsibility to lead his family to Christ and in Christ. Unless the churches begin to reestablish small group relationships and train men to lead these, evangelizing the individual will be increasingly unfruitful.

The conditions are radically different, both in England and America, than they were when revival and evangelism were so effective in the eighteenth and nineteenth centuries. Until late in the nineteenth century the institutions of America were committed to the Christian philosophy of life. Eighty-five percent of the colleges and universities were teaching Christian theism until after the Civil War. Since that time secular humanism as a religion has been more clearly formulated and has become the dominant philosophy in our colleges and universities. It has permeated the mass media, the legal, governmental, and especially the judicial systems, and has undermined Christian ethics. In the eighteenth and nineteenth centuries the controlling Christian philosophy in the institutions was a background to give credibility to revival preaching. Today that no longer is true; secular humanism is in control. Moreover, far too much evangelism has been only a reemphasis of the individual's importance without leading him into social responsibilities in the family and church.

Evangelism and missions are still needed in the churches, but they are no longer the main need. Evangelism and missions extend the church, but the Christian family perpetuates or continues the church. The great commission of Christ involves not only making disciples of all nations but also "teaching them to *observe* all things" Christ commanded (Matthew 28:19,20). Application of truth must be made in the family.

Unless the Christian family is strong and reproduces the believing community, the gains of evangelism and missions will not be real gains. If the main tree catches a disease and is in danger of being destroyed in any way, what benefit is it for the tree to put forth new branches and buds? If the family that gives continuance to the church goes, evangelism and missions will die too.

We have shown that in the eighteenth century, when the great evangelistic thrust began with the Great Awakening, only five to six percent of the American people were in the churches, whereas today about two-thirds of them are church members. When the great American missionary movement began in the late nineteenth century, only a small fraction of the world had been evangelized. Literally thousands of American young men and women went to the mission fields in the first half of the twentieth century because of the influence of the Student Volunteer Movement and the Foreign Missions Fellowship. World evangelism has continued even after the withdrawal of the West from a dominant colonial position, which began about 1945. Today a vital national church exists in most countries of the world.[1]

But even though membership in the churches of America has grown, secular humanism has diminished the vitality of the educational program of the church. It has especially weakened the family structure and is in fact destroying the family. While no church can remain vital without evangelism and missions, the main focus must now turn toward discipleship and the family. Also, even though many churches are being established throughout the world, the third-world churches have tended to catch the diseases of the American church because they often follow American models. The American emphasis on material wealth and success in numbers and programs is spreading, and secular humanism is affecting the family worldwide. This focus on discipleship and the family is needed worldwide.

While more mass evangelism, personal evangelism, television preaching, teaching of correct Bible doctrine, and other similar efforts are needed, they are not likely to bring widespread renewal. *There have been more of these in the past twenty years than ever before, but the rate of moral decline in the nation has increased.* I believe these measures have been beneficial, but our energies even through these would better be redirected and more clearly focused on bringing renewal at the source of the problem, namely, in producing genuine change in regard to values men hold and man's spiritual leadership of the home. I believe a change of women's views and actions toward the home would follow.

True renewal has always aimed at removing idolatry

and renewing the family. Israel forgot God's laws and He did not bless their children (Hosea 4:6). Malachi predicted the revival of the nation would come when Elijah the prophet would "restore the hearts of the fathers to their children, and the hearts of the children to their fathers" (Malachi 4:6). John the Baptist did this in his preaching in preparing them to receive Christ (Luke 1:17).

The Way of Previous Renewal:
National Male Commitment

But how then can a powerful movement be set in motion to change the family and promote national renewal?

There have been biblical precedents in producing spiritual and moral renewal, especially in Judah, that can point the way to go. The nation of Judah had periodic spiritual renewals that enabled it to last 135 years longer than its northern sister nation of Israel, which did not have renewal.

These renewals occurred by calling the men to commit themselves to a specifically written covenant with God in a great public gathering. The covenants usually pointed to specific areas for obedience where they had been failing. The men were required to come together for this purpose on one of the three major religious holidays—either the Passover, Pentecost or the Feast of Tabernacles. God had commanded that all men gather in Jerusalem on those occasions.

Such a covenant of renewal was agreed to and had good and often longlasting effects. We see this occurring under Joshua (Joshua 24:13–25,31), Asa (2 Chronicles 15:1–16), Hezekiah (2 Chronicles 29:1–11; 30:1–14; 30:25–31:1), Josiah (2 Chronicles 34:29–35:1) and others.

Each of these times of renewal was promoted by a leader or king who led the men to make the covenant with God, and then he followed it up by actually enforcing the removal of the idols of worship and by promoting local training as to what the will of God was.

Such a public gathering and renewal of a covenant with God would help renew the national civil religion and would unite the churches in a vital thrust in the right direction of motivating their men to be trained and become leaders of their homes.

Objections to this Approach Today

Many say that such a covenant cannot be used today. Some say Jesus forbids His people, in Matthew 5:33–37, from making any covenant, since a covenant is a form of an oath. Any exposition of that passage of Scripture must recognize that He was speaking against abuses of the old covenant laws in which they were outwardly claiming to obey the laws but inwardly were disobeying them. They outwardly rejected murder but inwardly were angry with their brothers, and they outwardly rejected adultery but lusted in their hearts. The Jews were swearing oaths vociferously and insistently as if outwardly they were being honest, while inwardly they were dishonest. Jesus therefore called His disciples to heart honesty which could say "yes" or "no" and mean it. Requiring an oath when there was no intention of keeping it was excluded as an option for them. But Jesus did not mean no oath should ever be made.

Jesus Himself led His disciples to form a covenant with Him. At the celebration of the Passover the night before His death Jesus said, "This is my blood of the covenant which is to be shed on behalf of many" (Mark 14:24; Luke 22:14–20; Matthew 26:26–28). When they drank the cup they were entering into a covenant with Him.

The Apostle Paul took a vow (Acts 18:18; 21:23), and he swore an oath two times in his epistles to churches (cf. Galatians 1:20; 2 Corinthians 11:31).

The Old Testament marriage covenant was practiced by early Christians and is still practiced today. Hence, to make a covenant or swear an oath was not excluded for Christians.

Others point out that there is no unified leader or king who can lead such a renewal today. This is a significant difference, but there are other advantages to compensate. Jesus Christ is the Head of all Christians, and He works in the hearts and heads of all of them by His Holy Spirit. This did not exist in the Old Testament. It should be remembered that had not God in the Old Testament moved the people to respond to the king's call to attend the covenant meeting, there would have been no revival (2 Chronicles 30:12). Jesus, the King of the church, can call His people to respond. Since two-thirds of the American people are related to the churches today, the churches have access to the people as never before.

The movement today must come by way of a demand from the multitudes of believing Christians as Christ moves them through the Spirit. And today, because of modern technology, communication to all believers worldwide is possible. The modern airmail system with computers to record and help transmit, modern printing methods, television, radio, and the like, make it possible to reach the Christians of the world.

Why We Can Expect a Movement Toward Covenant Renewal Today

Jeremy Rifkin and Ted Howard, in their recent book *The Emerging Order,* argue that the liberal philosophy which aims at material progress and expansion by man's scientific and technological genius is now antiquated and dying and must be replaced by some new philosophy of covenant with God. They present evidence from public opinion polls, legislative trends, political trends, reactions to governmental failures (e.g., Watergate) and confusion to support their theses. They present facts to show that mankind is facing material limitations and that continued progress, growth, and expansion is impossible. The end of nonrenewable resources such as oil, coal, minerals, et al., required for an industrialized civilization is fast approaching.[2] This was convincingly shown by Harrison Brown, noted California Tech scientist, as early as 1954.[3] The availability and distribution of food for an increasing world population is rapidly becoming inadequate. Pollution is "closing in on us from all directions with exponential speed and force."[4]

I have pointed out in my book *With Christ in the School of Disciple Building* that the developments of secular studies in recent years have shown that the very foundations of the liberal philosophy that were so convincing in leading people to reject faith in God for hope in man's ability to build a material heaven on earth were based on many fallacious assumptions and distortions of facts.[5]

Therefore the world is having its philosophical house swept clean, and unless there is genuine spiritual renewal to restore real faith in God, it will take in seven demons worse than that now possessing it. Rifkin and Howard show that there is an urgent need for a spiritual covenant, and that neo-evangelical and charismatic Christians are the growing influence in the United States. Such biblically oriented Christians are building huge systems for communication by radio and television, a powerful network of private schools, and a culture that can have a powerful impact on America if these religious groups can present the right covenant philosophy.[6]

The whole world is beginning to look for a spiritual answer. This is indicated by the resurgence of emphasis on the Moslem religion in the Near East (e.g., Iran, et al.) and the great crowds that have attended the travels of the pope recently. The United States seems especially ready and prepared by God for a renewal of a covenant relationship to Him.

Four Things Needed to Achieve Genuine Renewal

Four main things will have to be achieved to make such a covenant effective:

1. *Prayer* for Christ to speak to believers' hearts and motivate them to do this.
2. *Personal Commitment* to accept and keep the covenant and to promote its acceptance by others.
3. Attendance at a *National Rally* to make the commitment to the covenant public so that it will call the nation to the ideals. This might be preceded by local rallies.
4. *Training* of each member of the covenant so that
   a. they can learn how to be an effective father or mother and
   b. they can grow to maturity, whereby they can fulfill the responsibilities of the covenant.

What You Can Do As An Individual

The first three of these can be achieved primarily by *you* and others like you. Begin daily praying for this renewal and also sign the covenant agreement. Then seek to get at least three others to pray and sign it. Loan your copy of this book to five others or order five other copies of this book, give them to friends, and urge them to read it and sign the covenant. Talk to those who don't like to read and explain what is involved and seek to get them to sign it. Mail the cards of those who sign the covenant to this publisher. If each person who reads the book does this, then a growing wave of commitment to family renewal will take place and *you* will be a major cause.

Suppose you gave five books to friends and encouraged them to commit themselves to do as you have, and three of them did it. If the three likewise gave five and three responded, there would be 13. As this procedure continues, rapid multiplication will occur. If this occurred every week for 13 weeks, *you* alone would have gained the commitment of 2,391,484 people! Even with much less efficiency, it would not take long to involve a very large number of people in America.

After a large number of people in a given geographic area sign the covenant, they could be brought together for a meeting to accelerate promotion of the covenant and to plan and promote the attendance at a local rally, then a regional rally and then at a national rally to make a declaration of family ideals to the whole nation. More details about the covenant idea and how to promote this can be obtained from the publisher of this book. You will be advised about plans for the national rally and about what more can be done locally and regionally.

Training to Meet Responsibilities and Build Disciples

As pastors and capable laymen respond, those who want help will be gathered for seminars and taught how to train the laymen in their church or area in how to be effective parents. Also, they will be trained to disciple these laymen and help them to grow spiritually to be mature enough to assume the responsibilities of an effective marriage partner and parent. Worldwide Discipleship Association is preparing such training and can suggest other resources to those desiring it. Denominational leaders can promote this as well.

Chapter 17

SUGGESTED COVENANTS TO SIGN

Following are covenant agreements for married men, married women, single men, and single women. Choose the one appropriate for you, prayerfully read and sign it. Then fill in the card and mail it immediately. (Single copies of the card and covenants can be ordered from the publisher.)

MARRIED MAN'S COVENANT WITH CHRIST

I hereby confess my trust in You, Lord Jesus, and renew my covenant of obedience to you because of Your love for me. I acknowledge You as a personal disclosure of the trinitarian God, revealed as the Son sent from the eternal Father, and with the Father, the sender of the Holy Spirit. I believe You died for my sins, were raised from the dead, and are exalted to all authority in heaven and on earth. I submit to You as the Lord and Governor over the world, and in this age especially over the church. I hereby recommit myself to obey You particularly in regard to establishing Your rule in and through the family in the following matters:

1. As a man, I believe I am called by You, Lord Jesus, to be the head and leader of my home. I accept this office, not as one for selfish special privilege, but as one under obligation to know, teach, and exemplify Your will. I therefore pledge myself to seek to show the same sacrificial servant love for my wife and children as You showed for the church when You gave Yourself for it.
2. I believe my wife is equally made in God's image, equally belonging to You, destined to be an heir with me in heaven, but now called to be my helper in conceiving, bearing, training, and providing for children for the glory of God. I will aim at being my wife's partner and friend in life and I commit myself to seek to understand her needs and to help her de-

velop spiritually, mentally, and physically as I would desire to develop myself.

3. I believe You have created sex for the procreation of children and for lovingly bestowing pleasure on my wife as well as for my personal enjoyment. Accepting personal forgiveness for past failures, I hereby commit myself to sexual fidelity to my wife, both in thought and act, and to life-long monogamous marriage.

4. I believe that having children and training them to trust and obey You is one of the most important ways of extending Your kingdom on earth. I hereby commit myself, with my wife, to make it a priority to spend time and effort to love and train our children for the glory of God.

5. I confess that the men of America have grievously sinned in putting personal success, achievement, and wealth above being Your minister to our wives and children. I commit myself in the future to trust Your promise that if I seek first Your kingdom and righteousness, You will provide all things we need. I interpret that seeking Your kingdom first involves working hard six days at the task to which You call me, and trusting You by completely resting and worshiping You one day. The object of my productive labor will be to provide for my family, to help others in need, and to extend your kingdom.

6. I believe in the importance of the individual and one's rights before God, but I believe the worth and freedom of the individual are developed and protected best when society is promoted by voluntarily giving up freedom for responsible service to others—first in the family, then in the church, in industry, and in government. I therefore commit myself to support all efforts to promote social responsibility, while at the same time holding to the value and freedom of

the individual. But I also commit myself, within the law, to oppose as anarchistic all religious, educational, mass-media, and governmental efforts to place individual rights above those of society, especially of the family.

7. I believe that my human responsibility is to love God with my whole person and my neighbor as You loved me and gave Yourself for me. Such love is specifically defined by You in the Ten Commandments and is supremely manifested in Your life and death. Even though I am free from the judgment by the law, the Ten Commandments express Your will, so I commit myself to keep them, both in thought and deed, and to aim at becoming like You, Jesus Christ. I also commit myself to teach my family to do likewise. I acknowledge that I cannot live obediently in my own power, but only through the indwelling strength the Holy Spirit gives and with the help of the Christian community.

8. I believe that the effect of this covenant commitment upon me (and our nation) will depend upon my seeking Your help through Scripture and prayer and through the church and its leadership. I therefore commit myself to seek the help of my church leaders in order to grow to spiritual maturity and to be trained to be an effective husband and father as is required in the Bible.

9. I believe that You are the Lord of the whole church and that You wish to unite Your people to renew the family, the church, the educational system, and the nation. I therefore commit myself to support the movement to call men and their families together to promote renewal with such time, prayer, effort and money as God leads and enables me. I do this because I believe this movement will strengthen the whole kingdom of God and therefore my own particu-

lar church. Hence, my support will be given in such ways and as long as it achieves those objectives. I also promise to promote such unity without imposing my distinctive views on my brethren.

10. I make this covenant voluntarily and in good conscience before You, knowing that the values and moral principles of this covenant are at variance with those of the modern secular humanistic world and that therefore it may lead to opposition, ridicule and suffering. I commit myself to You, Lord Jesus, to do Your will in these matters, as You were obedient to the Father even unto death. I do so knowing that You offer eternal life and rewards to those who trust You.

SIGNED _____

ADDRESS _____

_____

DATE _____

Please sign and mail the card at the back of this book.

MARRIED WOMAN'S COVENANT WITH CHRIST

I hereby confess my trust in You, Lord Jesus, and renew my covenant of obedience to You because of Your love for me. I acknowledge You as a personal disclosure of the trinitarian God, revealed as the Son sent from the eternal Father, and, with the Father, the sender of the Holy Spirit. I believe You died for my sins, were raised from the dead, and are exalted to all authority in heaven and on earth. I submit to You as the Lord and Governor over the world, and in this age especially over the church. I hereby recommit myself to obey You particularly in regard to establishing Your rule in and through the family in the following matters:

1. As a woman, I believe I am equally created in the image of God as is the man and a joint heir to eternal life, but that I am different from him in nature and purpose. I believe that as a wife I am called to be my husband's helper in personal matters and also in conceiving, bearing, training, and providing for our children for the glory of God.

2. I accept my husband as Your official leader in our home and I promise to seek to respect and submit to him in everything as I would to You. I will aim at being my husband's partner and friend in life. I will seek to communicate freely with him but not to contend with him when I differ. If he fails to be the loving leader You intended, I will love him and quietly

suffer wrong for Your sake, looking to You in prayer to change him.

3. I believe You have created sex for the procreation of children and that bearing and raising children is a high and holy calling which is important for building the kingdom of God. I believe that sex was also created for pleasure, which I can give to my husband and also enjoy myself. Accepting forgiveness for any past failures in thought or deed, I hereby commit myself to faithfulness to my husband alone and to life-long monogamous marriage.

4. I confess that many women have sinned in following non-Christian values of male leadership in putting financial gain, personal prominence, and pleasure above the home. I believe all women have the capability and right to serve in various vocations, but I believe that as a wife, my work and abilities should be first aimed at helping my husband lead our family in following You and in providing for their needs. Hence, I covenant to take a servant role of helping and honoring him and will seek personal fulfillment in using my abilities first in that way and secondarily for myself.

5. I believe in the importance of the individual and one's rights before God, but I believe the worth and freedom of the individual are developed and protected best when society is promoted by voluntarily giving up freedom for responsible service to others—first in the family, then in the church, in industry, and in government. I therefore commit myself to support all efforts to promote social responsibility, while at the same time holding to the value and freedom of the individual. But I also commit myself, within the law, to oppose as anarchistic all religious, educational, mass media, and governmental efforts to place individual rights above those of society, especially of the family.

6. I believe that my human responsibility is to love God

with my whole person and my neighbor as You loved me and gave Yourself for me. Such love is specifically defined by You in the Ten Commandments and is supremely manifested in Your life and death. Even though I am free from judgment by the law, the Ten Commandments express Your will, so I therefore commit myself to keep them, both in thought and deed, and to aim at becoming like You, Jesus Christ. I also commit myself to teach my family to do likewise. I acknowledge that I cannot live obediently in my own power, but only through the indwelling strength the Holy Spirit gives and with the help of the Christian community.

7. I believe that the effect of this covenant commitment upon me (and our nation) will depend upon my seeking Your help through Scripture and prayer and through the church and its leadership. I therefore commit myself to seek the help of my husband and my church leaders in order to grow to spiritual maturity and to be trained to be an effective wife and mother as is required in the Bible.

8. I believe that You are the Lord of the whole church and that You wish to unite Your people to renew the family, the church, the educational system, and the nation. I therefore commit myself to support the movement to call Your people together to promote renewal with such time, prayer, effort and money as God leads and enables me. I do this because I believe this movement will strengthen the whole kingdom of God and therefore my own particular church. Hence, my support will be given in such ways and as long as it achieves those objectives. I also promise to promote such unity without imposing my distinctive views on my brethren.

9. I make this covenant voluntarily and in good conscience before You, knowing that the values and moral

principles of this covenant are at variance with those of the modern secular humanistic world and that therefore it may lead to opposition, ridicule and suffering. I commit myself to You, Lord Jesus, to do Your will in these matters, as You were obedient to the Father even unto death. I do so knowing that You offer eternal life and rewards to those who trust You.

SIGNED _____

ADDRESS _____

_____

    DATE _____

Please sign and mail the card at the back of this book.

SINGLE MAN'S COVENANT WITH CHRIST

I hereby confess my trust in You, Lord Jesus, and renew my covenant of obedience to You because of Your love for me. I acknowledge You as a personal disclosure of the trinitarian God, revealed as the Son sent from the eternal Father, and, with the Father, the sender of the Holy Spirit. I believe You died for my sins, were raised from the dead, and are exalted to all authority in heaven and on earth. I submit to You as the Lord and Governor over the world, and in this age especially over the church. I hereby recommit myself to obey You particularly in regard to establishing Your rule in and through the family in the following matters.

1. Most men normally will be called by You to marry and be the head and leader of their home. If I marry, I promise to accept this office, not as one for selfish special privilege, but as one under obligation to know, teach, and exemplify Your will. I therefore pledge myself to seek to establish a Christian home and to show the same sacrificial servant love for my wife and children as You showed for the church when You gave Yourself for it.

2. I believe women are equally made in God's image, destined to be heirs with men in heaven. But now in this life I believe, that as a wife, the woman is called to be a helper in conceiving, bearing, training, and providing for children for the glory of God. I promise to treat my wife as my partner and friend

in life and I commit myself to seek to understand her needs and to help her develop spiritually, mentally, and physically as I desire to develop myself. I therefore promise to seek a woman of God for a wife, one who will desire to be my helper in these ways.

3. If You do not call me to marriage, I promise to treat other women as sisters in Christ. I recognize that some Christian women will be called to serve in various vocations without marrying, and I promise to support, protect, and encourage these in their Christian life, treating them as equal in value before God.

4. I believe You have created sex for the procreation of children and for lovingly bestowing pleasure on the wife as well as for the husband's personal enjoyment. Accepting personal forgiveness for past failures, I hereby commit myself to sexual purity both in thought and act until marriage and to fidelity to my wife after marriage. I also pledge myself to support life-long monogamous marriage.

5. I believe that having children and training them to trust and obey You is one of the most important ways of extending God's kingdom on earth. I hereby commit myself to make it a priority, with my future wife, to spend time and effort to love and train our children for the glory of God.

6. I confess that the men of America have grievously sinned in putting personal success, achievement, and wealth above being God's minister to their wives and children. I commit myself in the future to trust Your promise that if I seek first Your kingdom and righteousness, You will provide all things I and my family will need. I interpret that seeking Your kingdom first involves working hard six days at the task to which You call me, and trusting You by completely resting and worshiping You one day.

7. I believe in the importance of the individual and one's

rights before God, but I believe the worth and freedom of the individual are developed and protected
best when society is promoted by voluntarily giving
up freedom for responsible service to others—first
in the family, then in the church, in industry, and
in government. I therefore commit myself to support
all efforts to promote social responsibility, while at
the same time holding to the value and freedom of
the individual. But I also commit myself, within the
law, to oppose as anarchistic all religious, educational,
mass media, and governmental efforts to place individual rights above those of society, especially of the
family.

8. I believe that my human responsibility is to love God
with my whole person and my neighbor as You loved
me and gave Yourself for me. Such love is specifically
defined by You in the Ten Commandments and is
supremely manifested in Your life and death. Even
though I am free from judgment by the law, because
the Ten Commandments express Your will, so I therefore commit myself to keep them, both in thought
and deed, and to aim at becoming like You, Jesus
Christ. I also commit myself to teach my family to
do likewise. I acknowledge that I cannot live obediently in my own power, but only through the indwelling strength the Holy Spirit gives and with the help
of the Christian community.

9. I believe that the effect of this covenant commitment
upon me (and our nation) will depend upon my seeking Your help through Scripture and prayer and
through the church and its leadership. I therefore
commit myself to seek the help of my church leaders
in order to grow to spiritual maturity and to be
trained to be an effective man, whether as single or
as a husband and father, as is required in the Bible.

10. I believe that You are the Lord of the whole church

and that You wish to unite Your people to renew the family, the church, the educational system, and the nation. I therefore commit myself to support the movement to call Your people together to promote renewal with such time, prayer, effort and money as God leads and enables me. I do this because I believe this movement will strengthen the whole kingdom of God and therefore my own particular church. Hence, my support will be given in such ways and as long as it achieves those objectives. I also promise to promote such unity without imposing my distinctive views on my brethren.

11. I make this covenant voluntarily and in good conscience before You, knowing that the values and moral principles of this covenant are at variance with those of the modern secular humanistic world and that therefore it may lead to opposition, ridicule and suffering. I commit myself to You, Lord Jesus, to do Your will in these matters, as You were obedient to the Father even unto death. I do so knowing that You offer eternal life and rewards to those who trust You.

SIGNED _____

ADDRESS _____

_____

DATE _____

Please sign and mail the card at the back of this book.

SINGLE WOMAN'S COVENANT WITH CHRIST

I hereby confess my trust in You, Lord Jesus, and renew my covenant of obedience to You because of Your love for me. I acknowledge You as a personal disclosure of the trinitarian God, revealed as the Son sent from the eternal Father, and, with the Father, the sender of the Holy Spirit. I believe You died for my sins, were raised from the dead, and are exalted to all authority in heaven and on earth. I submit to You as the Lord and Governor over the world, and in this age especially over the church. I hereby recommit myself to obey You particularly in regard to establishing Your rule in and through the family in the following matters:

1. As a woman, I believe I am equally created in the image of God as is the man and a joint heir to eternal life, but that I am different from him in nature and purpose. I believe that if God gives me a husband, I will be called to be his helper in personal matters and also in conceiving, bearing, training, and providing for children for the glory of God.

2. I promise to accept my future husband as Your official leader in our home and to seek to respect him and submit to him in everything. I will aim at being his partner and friend in life and I will seek to communicate freely with him but not to contend with him when I differ. If he fails to be the loving leader You intended, I will love him and quietly suffer wrong for Your sake, looking to You in prayer to change

him. As a single woman I promise to seek to develop the attitudes of respect and honor toward men so that I may better prepare myself to serve You under the leadership of my husband and/or the leaders of the church. I also promise that I will look to You to provide me with a godly, loving husband with whom I can serve. I will submit myself to the leadership counsel of my father until such time as you give me a Christian husband.

3. I believe You have created sex for the procreation of children and that bearing and raising children is God's high and holy calling for most women. It is important for building the kingdom of God. If I marry I promise to prayerfully look to You to enable me to bear and raise children for You. I believe that sex was also created for pleasure, which I can first give to my husband and also enjoy myself. Accepting forgiveness for any past failures in thought or deed, I hereby commit myself to sexual purity until marriage, then to faithfulness to my future husband alone and to life-long monogamous marriage.

4. I confess that many women have sinned in following non-Christian values of male leadership in putting financial gain, personal prominence, and pleasure above the home. I believe all women have the capability and right to serve in various vocations, but I believe that when I become a wife my work and abilities should be first aimed at helping my husband lead our family in following You and in providing for their needs. Hence, I covenant to take a servant role of helping and honoring him and will seek personal fulfillment in using my abilities first in that way.

5. As a single woman I will seek to develop my skills and abilities so that I can fulfill God's calling for me, and if that is in marriage I will be the greatest possible help to my future husband. Should I not

marry I will use them to the glory of God as a single woman.

6. I believe in the importance of the individual and one's rights before God, but I believe the worth and freedom of the individual are developed and protected best when society is promoted by voluntarily giving up freedom for responsible service to others—first in the family, then in the church, in industry, and in government. I therefore commit myself to support all efforts to promote social responsibility, while at the same time holding to the value and freedom of the individual. But I also commit myself, within the law, to oppose as anarchistic all religious, educational, mass media, and governmental efforts to place individual rights above those of society, especially of the family.

7. I believe that my human responsibility is to love God with my whole person and my neighbor as You loved me and gave Yourself for me. Such love is specifically defined by You in the Ten Commandments and is supremely manifested in Your life and death. Even though I am free from judgment by the law, the Ten Commandments express Your will, so I therefore commit myself to keep them, both in thought and deed, and to aim at becoming like You, Jesus Christ. I also commit myself to teach my family to do likewise. I acknowledge that I cannot live obediently in my own power, but only through the indwelling strength the Holy Spirit gives and with the help of the Christian community.

8. I believe that the effect of this covenant commitment upon me (and our nation) will depend upon my seeking Your help through Scripture and prayer and through the church and its leadership. I therefore commit myself to seek the help of my church leaders in order to grow to spiritual maturity and to be

trained to be an effective woman, whether as single
or as a wife and mother, as is required in the Bible.

9. I believe that You are the Lord of the whole church
   and that You wish to unite Your people to renew
   the family, the church, the educational system, and
   the nation. I therefore commit myself to support the
   movement to call Your people together to promote
   renewal with such time, prayer, effort and money
   as God leads and enables me. I do this because I
   believe this movement will strengthen the whole kingdom of God and therefore my own particular church.
   Hence, my support will be given in such ways and
   as long as it achieves those objectives. I also promise
   to promote such unity without imposing my distinctive views on my brethren.

10. I make this covenant voluntarily and in good con-
    science before You, knowing that the values and
    moral principles of this covenant are at variance with
    those of the modern secular humanistic world and
    that therefore it may lead to opposition, ridicule and
    suffering. I commit myself to You, Lord Jesus, to
    do Your will in these matters, as You were obedient
    to the Father even unto death. I do so knowing that
    You offer eternal life and rewards to those who trust
    You.

SIGNED _____

ADDRESS _____

_____

Copyright 1979
by Carl W. Wilson   DATE _____

Please sign and mail the card at the back of this book.

NOTES

CHAPTER 1

[1] Norman Cousins, *In God We Trust* (New York: Harper and Row, 1958), p. 42.

[2] Cf. J. Edwin Orr, *Campus Aflame* (Glendale, Calif.: Regal Books, 1971), pp. 25–37.

[3] See Edward M. Deems, *Holy Days and Holidays* (New York: Funk and Wagnalls, 1901), pp. 340–344.

[4] Winthrop S. Hudson, "Fast Days and Civil Religion," in Winthrop S. Hudson and Leonard J. Trinterud, *Theology in Sixteenth and Seventeenth Century England* (Los Angeles: U. C. L. A. William Andrews Clark Memorial Library, 1971), p. 6.

[5] For a one-sided but documented story of abuse, see Dee Brown, *Bury My Heart at Wounded Knee* (New York: Bantam Books, 1971).

[6] Hudson and Trinterud, p. 5.

[7] Pitirim Sorokin, *The Crisis of Our Age* (New York: E. P. Dutton, 1941), p. 247.

CHAPTER 2

[1] Pitirim Sorokin, *The American Sex Revolution* (Boston: Porter Sargent, 1956); and *The Crisis of Our Age.*

[2] Sorokin, *The American Sex Revolution,* p. 5.

[3] Michael Novak, "The Family is the Future," from *Harper's,* April, 1976, condensed in *Reader's Digest,* March, 1978, p. 111.

[4] W. G. Forrest, *The Emergence of Greek Democracy* (New York: McGraw-Hill, 1966), pp. 50–58. Cf. also H. D. F. Kitto, *The Greeks* (Baltimore: Pelican Books, 1951), pp. 12–28; and J. H. Vincent and J. R. Joy, *An Outline History of Greece* (New York: Chautauga Press, 1888), pp. 17–22.

[5] J. H. Vincent and J. R. Joy, *An Outline History of Rome* (New York: Chautauga Press, 1889), pp. 32–59.

[6] Thomas Jefferson Wertenbaker, *The Puritan Oligarchy: The Founding of American Civilization* (New York: Grosset and Dunlap, 1947), pp. 41–77.

[7] Arthur Calhoun, *The Social History of the American Family, Vol. I: Colonial Period* (New York: Barnes and Noble, 1960), pp. 75, 76.

[8] Cf. Ibid., pp. 72, 74.

[9] Robert Middlekauff, *The Mathers: Three Generations of Puritan Intellectuals, 1596–1728* (New York: Oxford University Press, 1971).

[10] Novak, p. 113.

[11] The White House Conference on Children, United States Government Printing Office, 1970, p. 25 and p. 10.

[12] Armand M. Nicholi II, "The Fractured Family: Following it into the Future," *Christianity Today,* May 25, 1979, pp. 11–15.

CHAPTER 3

[1a] Dr. Paul Popenoe, "Are Women Really Different?" *Family Life,* February 1971, Vol. XXXI, No. 2.

[1b] Herbert J. Miles, *Sexual Happiness in Marriage* (Grand Rapids: Zondervan, 1967), p. 89.

[2] Dr. Marie Robinson, *The Power of Sexual Surrender* (New York: Signet Books, 1959), pp.19–27.

[3] George Gilder, *Sexual Suicide* (New York: Bantam Books, 1975), pp. 17,18.

[4] Seymour Fisher, *Understanding the Female Orgasm* (New York: Basic Books, 1973), p. 187.

[5] Gilder, pp. 19–21.

[6] Gilder, p. 20, taken from Mary Jane Sherfey, *The Nature and Evolution of Female Sexuality* (New York: Random House, 1972).

[7] Midge Dector, *The New Chastity and Other Arguments Against Women's Liberation* (New York: Coward, McCann and Geoghegan, 1972), p. 93.

[8] Marynia Farnham and Ferdinand Lundberg, *Modern Woman: The Lost Sex* (New York: Harper, 1947).

[9] Gilder, pp. 19,20.

[10] Clellan S. Ford and Frank A. Beach, *Patterns of Sexual Behavior* (New York: Harper & Row, 1951), pp. 95,257; cf. Gilder, pp. 22, 284.

[11] Robinson, p. 71.

[12] Gilder, p. 21.

[13] Richard M. Restak, "The Other Differences Between Boys and Girls," *Reader's Digest,* November, 1979, pp. 211–218, condensed from *The Brain: The Last Frontier* (New York: Doubleday and Co., 1979).

[14] Margaret Mead, "One Aspect of Male and Female," in *The Way of Women,* ed. J. E. Fairchild (New York: Fawcett, 1956), p. 21.

[15] Gilder, p. 26.

[16] Mead, in *The Way of Women,* p. 20.

[17] Cf. Sorokin, *The American Sex Revolution;* see chapter on "Creative Growth and Decay," pp. 106–130.

[18] Marynia Farnham, "The Lost Sex," in *The Way of Women,* p. 38.

[19] Gilder, p. 88.

[20] Ibid., p. 193.

[21] Ibid., p. 101.

[22] Margaret Mead, *Sex and Temperament in Three Primitive Societies*

(New York: Mentor Books, 1950); and *Male and Female* (New York: William Morrow, 1949), pp. 100, 101.

[23] Ralph Linton, "Women in the Family," in *The Way of Women,* p. 63.

[24] Judy Garland, "How Not to Love a Woman," *Reader's Digest,* May, 1955, pp. 115,116.

[25] Gilder, p. 246.

[26] Sarah Chakko and Kathleen Bliss, *A Study of Man-Woman Relationships* (London: S.C.M. Press, 1952), p. vii.

[27] Carolyn Lewis "A different Sort of Liberation," *New York Times,* December 5, 1977, reprinted in *Reader's Digest,* March, 1978, pp. 117, 118.

[28] Gilder, pp. 95–114.

[29] Ibid.

[30] See Farnham, in *The Way of Women,* p. 38; and her book *Modern Women: The Lost Sex.* Also cf. Gilder, "The Liberated Job Disaster," in *Sexual Suicide,* pp. 184–197.

[31] Judge Samuel S. Leibowitz, "Nine Words to End Juvenile Delinquency," *This Week,* December 15, 1957 (New York: United Newspaper Mag. Co.), reprinted in *Reader's Digest,* March, 1958, pp. 105 ff.

[32] Ashley Montagu, *The Humanization of Man* (Cleveland: World Publishing Co., 1962); cf. *Reader's Digest,* February, 1963.

[33] Urie Bronfenbrenner, *Two Worlds of Childhood: U. S. and U. S. S. R.* (New York: Pocket Books, 1970), p. 120.

CHAPTER 4

[1] Wertenbaker, p. 68.

[2] Ibid., pp. 76, 77.

[3] See comments by William Warren Sweet, *The Story of Religion in America* (New York: Harper, 1950), p. 342.

[4] See what is probably the most objective study of conditions of the slaves—Robert W. Fogel and Stanley Engerman, *Time on the Cross* (Boston: Little, 1974).

[5] Cf. Rebecca Harding Davis and Tillie Olsen, *Life in the Iron Mills* (Old Westbury, New York: Feminist Press, 1973); and Calhoun, pp. 65–83.

[6] Sweet, p. 345 ff.

[7] Midge Yearley, "The Early American Women," *The Atlanta Journal and Constitution,* October 17, 1976.

[8] See "Declarations of Sentiments and Resolutions, Seneca Falls," in *Feminism: The Essential Historical Writings,* ed. Miriam Schneir (New York: Vantage Books, 1972), pp. 76–82.

[9] Mrs. William D. Sporborg, "Women as a Social Force," in *The Way of Women,* p. 164.

[10] *Life,* Special Issue, Vol. 41, No. 26, December 24, 1956, p. 109.

[11] Cleo Dawson, *The Rotarian,* September, 1957.

[12] George Gallup, "New Depth Study for the American Women," *Look,* Vol. 235, No. 46, p. 28.

[13] Mary Wollstonecraft, "A Vindication of the Rights of Women," in *Feminism: The Essential Historical Writings,* p. 85; and Claire Tomalin, *The Life and Death of Mary Wollstonecraft* (New York: Mentor Books, 1974), pp. 140 ff and 199 ff.

[14] Andrew Sinclair, *The Emancipation of the American Woman* (New York: Harper & Row, 1965), pp. 51, 52.

[15] Seymour Fisher, *The Female Orgasm: Psychology, Physiology, Fantasy* (New York: Basic Books, 1973). This is his more comprehensive study on this.

[16] Shere Hite, *The Hite Report* (New York: Dell Books, 1976), p. 436.

[17] Betty Friedan, *The Feminine Mystique* (New York: Dell, 1963).

[18] Kate Millett, *Sexual Politics* (Westminster, Md.: Doubleday, 1978).

[19] Bronfenbrenner, p. 106.

[20] Ben Stein, "The View from Sunset Boulevard," *Life,* Vol. 2, April, 1979, pp. 34–44; and Jim Walters, "The New Hollywood Hotshots," *U. S. News and World Report,* May 21, 1979, pp. 51, 52.

[21] Mead, in *The Way of Women,* p. 21.

[22] Farnham, in *The Way of Women,* p. 31.

[23] *Time,* August 21, 1970, p. 16.

[24] Sinclair, p. 47.

[25] Gloria Steinem in *Saturday Review of Education,* March, 1973.

[26] Kate Millett, *Sita* (New York: Farrar, Straus and Giroun, 1978).

[27] "Dr. David Reuben Answers Your Questions About Alternatives to Marriage," *McCall's,* February, 1972, p. 38.

[28] Margaret Mead, *Atlanta Journal,* July 26, 1976, as quoted from *The Washington Post.*

[29] Sorokin, *The American Sex Revolution,* p. 6.

[30] William H. Masters and Virginia E. Johnson, *Homosexuality in Perspective* (Boston: Little, Brown, 1979).

[31] Norman Hill, ed., *Free Sex: A Delusion* (New York: Popular Library, 1971), p. 9.

[32] Sorokin, *The American Sex Revolution,* pp. 69–73 on individual productivity and pp. 108–120 on social productivity.

[33] Robinson, pp. 48–67.

[34] Ann Landers, *The Atlanta Journal,* June 4, 1979.

[35] *Redbook,* Vol. 145, September, 1975, pp. 51–58.

[36] Fisher, *The Female Orgasm: Psychology, Physiology, Fantasy,* was referred to earlier, in footnote 15 of this chapter.

[37] Carol Botwin and Jerome L. Fine, "Is There Sex After Saying I Do?" *New York Times Magazine,* September 16, 1979, reprinted in *Reader's Digest,* February, 1980, pp. 91–94.

CHAPTER 5

[1] Charles Seltman, *Women in Antiquity* (London: Pan Books, 1956).

[2] Otto Kiefer, *Sexual Life in Ancient Rome* (New York: AMS Press, 1934), pp. 52 ff.

[3] B. A. G. Fuller, *A History of Philosophy* (New York: Henry Holt, 1945), p. 261.

[4] J. D. Unwin, *Sex and Culture* (London: Oxford University Press, 1939).

[5] See Sorokin, *The American Sex Revolution,* pp. 108–113.

CHAPTER 6

[1] Paul Vitz, *Psychology as Religion: The Cult of Self-Worship* (Grand Rapids: Eerdmans, 1977).

[2] William E. Simon, *A Time for Truth* (New York: McGraw-Hill, 1978), pp. 63, 181, 212–214, 222.

[3] Source: Office of Management and Budget of the U. S. Government.

[4] See "Blacks in America: 25 years of Radical Change," *U. S. News & World Report,* May 14, 1979, pp. 48 ff, for most of these figures.

[5] Steve Dougherty, "Jackson," *The Atlanta Journal and Constitution,* September 8, 1979, p. 4A.

[6] Cf. Ronald J. Sider, *Rich Christians in an Age of Hunger* (Downers Grove, Illinois: Inter-Varsity Press, 1977), pp. 40, 41.

[7] "New Breed of Workers," *U. S. News & World Report,* September 3, 1979, pp. 35–38.

[8] Ibid., pp. 35,36.

[9] Ibid., p. 36.

[10] Ibid., p. 38.

[11] Bob Dant, *The Atlanta Journal and Constitution,* September 3, 1979.

[12] John Underwood, "Football's Unfolding Tragedy," from *Sports Illustrated,* condensed in *Reader's Digest,* September, 1979, p. 90–97. Cf. James Michener, *Sports in America* (New York: Random House, 1976).

[13] Kevin Phillips, "The Balkanization of America," *Harper's,* May, 1978.

[14] "The 'Rights' Explosion Splintering America?", *U. S. News & World Report,* October 31, 1977, p. 29.

[15] "The Losing Battle Against Crime in America," *U. S. News & World Report,* December 16, 1974, pp. 30, 31.

[16] Cf. Hill, *Free Sex: A Delusion;* Vance Packard, *The Sexual Wilderness* (New York: Pocket Books, 1970); and George Paul Csicsery, ed., *The Sex Industry* (New York: Signet Books, 1973).

[17] Dr. Albert Ellis, *Sex and the Single Man* (New York: Lyle Stuart, Dell Books, 1963).

18 Helen Gurley Brown, *Sex and the Single Girl* (New York: Pocket Books, 1962).

19 Hite, pp. 199, 200.

20 Robinson, pp. 40–58.

21 Roger Longley and Richard Levy, *Wife Beating: The Silent Crisis* (New York: Dutton, 1977). Cf. also "Battered Families: A Growing Nightmare," *U. S. News & World Report,* January 15, 1979, p. 60, which reports violence in one-half of all American families.

22 Donald Lambro, "Sexual Harrassment Common in HUD Offices," United Press release in *Atlanta Journal,* July 27, 1979, p. 1A.

23 Nathan M. Adams, "Why the Shocking Rise in Prostitution?", *Reader's Digest,* May, 1978, pp. 203–210.

24 See preview of their book in *The Atlanta Journal,* January 30, 1978.

25 Warrick and Zekman, "Risky Abortions," *Time,* November, 1978.

26 "Working Women," *U. S. News and World Report,* January 15, 1979, pp. 64–68.

27 Patricia McCormack, United Press release in *The Atlanta Journal,* October 2, 1978.

28 Gilder, p. 268.

29 Ted Howard and Jeremy Rifkin, *Who Should Play God?* (New York: Dell, 1977), p. 88.

30 Gilder, p. 275.

31 Ibid., p. 273.

32 Howard and Rifkin, pp. 47–82.

33 Ibid., pp. 75,76.

34 Ibid., p. 94.

35 See B. F. Skinner, *Beyond Freedom and Dignity* (New York: Knopf, 1971).

36 Howard and Rifkin, p. 81.

37 Barbara A. Mikulski and Esther Laderer, *Ann Lander's Encyclopedia* (New York: Doubleday, 1978); United States Census; *U. S. News & World Report,* and others.

38 "On Unmarried Women," *Newsweek,* April 30, 1979, p. 71.

39 *U. S. News & World Report,* October 27, 1975, p. 32; cf. *Divorce, Child Custody, and Child Support, 1940–1978* (U. S. Department of Commerce, Bureau of Census, June, 1979), Special Studies Series No. 84, p. 23.

40 Urie Bronfenbrenner, *Readings in Social Psychology* (New York: Holt, Rinehart and Winston, 1958), p. 424; and *Two Worlds of Childhood,* pp. 102, 105, 109.

41 Bronfenbrenner, *Two Worlds of Childhood,* pp. 121–123. Cf. also Nicholi II, pp. 12–14, where he gives further data concerning the effects of missing parents, both mothers and fathers.

42 Nicholi, p. 11.

[43] The Pro-Family Forum, P. O. Box 14701, Fort Worth, Texas 76117. They report that The Women's International Democratic Foundation, whose quarterly journal is published in East Berlin, was responsible for the resolution for the International Women's Year and The International Year of the Child. For a more balanced view see Robert P. Dugan, Jr., "International Year of the Child," *Eternity,* September, 1979, p. 15.

[44] Robert Coles, *Children of Crisis,* 3 Vols. (Boston: Little, Brown, 1967–1971).

[45] Bronfenbrenner, *Two Worlds of Childhood,* pp. 119,120.

[46] See articles in *U. S. News & World Report,* September 5, 1977, p. 55; and September 12, 1977, p. 31. Cf. Onalee McGraw, *Secular Humanism and the School* (Washington: The Heritage Foundation, 1976).

[47] Franklin Zimring, Director of the University of Chicago's Center for Criminal Justice, claims this leveled off during the seventies. Eugene Doleschol, director of the National Council on Crime and Delinquency's Information Center, claims there has not been any increase in crime in recent years based on victimization census surveys for 1973–75. He believes it is all a delusion caused by better F. B. I. reporting. However, he himself says, "Homicide is the most accurately recorded of all crimes," and he admits the rate was 5 per 100,000 in the early 1960's and rose to 9.8 in 1974. Few policemen would agree with him, and a study is needed to evaluate the validity of the victimization studies.

[48] "Youth Gangs: They're Back, Growing Worse," *U. S. News & World Report,* August 20, 1979, p. 46.

[49] *Highlights from Drug Use Among American High School Students, 1975–1977,* pub. by U. S. Department of H. E. W.

[50] William Glasser, *The Identity Society* (New York: Harper and Row, 1976), p. 174.

[51] Ibid., p. 182.

[52] Ibid., pp. 184,185.

[53] John Leo, "Homosexuality: Tolerance vs. Approval," *Time,* January 8, 1979, pp. 48–51. Cf. also Seymour Fisher and Robert P. Greenberg, *The Scientific Credibility of Freud's Theories and Therapy* (New York: Basic Books, 1977); and Dr. Edmund Bengler, *Homosexuality: Disease or Way of Life?* (New York: Collier Books, 1962).

[54] Daniel Cappon, *Toward an Understanding of Homosexuality* (Englewood Cliffs, N. J.: Prentice-Hall, 1965), esp. the chapter entitled "The Sources of Homosexuality," pp. 67–111.

[55] Peter and Barbara Wyden, *Growing Up Straight* (New York: Stein and Day, 1968).

[56] John Leo, p. 48–51.

[57] Benjamin DeMott, "The Pro-Incest Lobby," Psychology Today, March 1980, pg. 11.

[58] Cf. her statements also in *U. S. News & World Report,* June 24, 1974.

CHAPTER 7

[1] Jan Lever, *Creation and Evolution* (Grand Rapids: Kregels Press, 1958), pp. 183–190.

[2] "7 Keys to Mormonism," *Reader's Digest* advertisement, April, 1979, 12-page insert.

[3] See "Mormonism," *Schaff-Herzogg Encyclopedia,* VIII, p. 11. Cf. Brigham Young's *Discourses.*

CHAPTER 13

[1] Bronfenbrenner, *Two Worlds of Childhood,* p. 95.

[2] Sorokin, *The American Sex Revolution,* p. 115.

[3] Cf. A. S. Makarenko, *The Road to Life* (Moscow: Foreign Language Publishing House, 1955).

[4] Bronfenbrenner, *Two Worlds of Childhood,* pp. 88, 91. Add Yuri Ryurikov, writing in the journal *Social Sciences,* says that parental neglect is worsening, especially by fathers. Viktor Perevedentsev says that open combat between Soviet couples is growing. Birthrate is also dropping. Already the divorce rate in the U. S. S. R. is one of every three marriages, ten percent of all births are illegitimate, and abortions are legal. They are about where the U. S. was ten years ago.

[5] "Honor Thy Mother," *Parents Magazine,* January, 1979, p. 32.

[6] Senator Sam Nunn, "The New Soviet Threat to NATO," *Reader's Digest,* July, 1977, pp. 73–77.

[7] John G. Hubbell, "Soviet Civil Defense: The Grim Realities," *Reader's Digest,* February, 1978.

[8] Congressional Office of Technology Assessment, study released May, 1979.

[9] *U. S. News & World Report,* September 5, 1977, pp. 18–24.

[10] Senator Sam Nunn of the Senate Armed Services Committee, in a release from his office dated February 9, 1979.

CHAPTER 14

[1] See Ronald H. Nash, "Three Kinds of Individualism," *Intercollegiate Review,* Fall, 1976, pp. 29–40.

[2] See William Heller, *The Rise of Puritanism* (Philadelphia: University of Pennsylvania Press, 1972), p. 171.

[3] On the extreme right have been groups headed by men such as Carl McIntyre and Billy James Hargis. On the left there are the National Council of Churches and the World Council of Churches, which have almost abandoned proclaiming the New Testament message of God's love in Christ for a political-social mission. See *Christianity Today*, February 2, 1979, pp. 54,55; Paul Ramsey, *Who Speaks for the Church?* (Nashville: Abingdon Press, 1967); and Ernest W. Lefever, *From Amsterdam to Nairobi: The World Council of Churches and The Third World* (1211 Connecticut Ave., Washington, D. C.: Ethics and Public Policy Center, 1979). The Roman Catholic Church, with its Vatican state, has long claimed the right to rule over or through governments in the name of Christ. Claiming to be the vicar of Christ on earth, popes have claimed the right to tell kings and presidents what to do. The blood of many of the religious wars in Europe was shed because of this. Neither Jesus, Paul, Peter nor any New Testament writer ever indicated the church should have direct political power like this.

[4] A. W. Tozer, *The Best of A. W. Tozer* (Grand Rapids: Baker Book House, 1978), p. 74.

CHAPTER 16

[1] Ralph Winter, *The Twenty-Five Unbelievable Years: 1945–1969* (South Pasadena: William Carey Library, 1970).

[2] Jeremy Rifkin and Ted Howard, *The Emerging Order* (New York: G. P. Putnam's Sons), 1979, pp. 3–96. I read their book after this book, *Our Dance Has Turned to Death*, had been turned over to the printer, but have added references to it because of its significance. Rifkin and Howard are good in the area of their specialty, which is business and economics. Their understanding of religious groups and religious history is incorrect and weak.

[3] Harrison Brown, *The Challenge of Man's Future* (New York: The Viking Press, 1954).

[4] Rifkin and Howard, *The Emerging Order*, p. 69.

[5] Carl W. Wilson, *With Christ in the School of Disciple Building* (Grand Rapids: Zondervan, 1976), pp. 41, 42.

[6] Rifkin and Howard, *The Emerging Order*, pp. 99–126.